Economic Reform Now

Economic Reform Now

A Global Manifesto to Rescue our Sinking Economies

*Heiner Flassbeck, Paul Davidson, James K. Galbraith,
Richard Koo, and Jayati Ghosh*

First published in 2013 by
PALGRAVE MACMILLAN®
in the United States—a division of St. Martin's Press LLC,
175 Fifth Avenue, New York, NY 10010.

Where this book is distributed in the UK, Europe and the rest of the world,
this is by Palgrave Macmillan, a division of Macmillan Publishers Limited,
registered in England, company number 785998, of Houndmills,
Basingstoke, Hampshire RG21 6XS.

Palgrave Macmillan is the global academic imprint of the above companies
and has companies and representatives throughout the world.

Palgrave® and Macmillan® are registered trademarks in the United States,
the United Kingdom, Europe and other countries.

ISBN: 978–1–137–36165–3

Library of Congress Cataloging-in-Publication Data

Flassbeck, Heiner.
    Economic reform now : a global manifesto to rescue our sinking
economies / Heiner Flassbeck, Paul Davidson, James K. Galbraith,
Richard Koo, and Jayati Ghosh.
        pages cm
    Includes bibliographical references.
    ISBN 978–1–137–36165–3 (alk. paper)
    1. Economic policy. 2. Global Financial Crisis, 2008–2009.
    3. International economic integration. I. Davidson, Paul, 1930–
    II. Title.
HD87.F583 2013
330—dc23   2013019046

A catalogue record of the book is available from the British Library.

Design by Newgen Knowledge Works (P) Ltd., Chennai, India.

First edition: October 2013

10 9 8 7 6 5 4 3 2 1

Printed in the United States of America.

Contents

List of Figures and Table   vii

Preface   ix

Chapter 1   Uncertainty and Austerity Policy   1
Paul Davidson

Chapter 2   New Thinking and a Strategic Policy
Agenda   23
James K. Galbraith

Chapter 3   Labor Markets and Economic Development   55
Heiner Flassbeck

Chapter 4   Balance Sheet Recessions and the Global
Economic Crisis   85
Richard Koo

Chapter 5   Economic Integration and Global Crises:
A Perspective from the Developing World   133
Jayati Ghosh

Chapter 6   Act Now! The Manifesto: A New Agenda
for Global Economic Policies   161
Jayati Ghosh

About the Authors 175

References 179

Figures and Table

Figures

3.1	Wage share and unemployment in the developed economies	61
4.1	Western economies in balance sheet recessions	89
4.2	Balance sheet recession in Japan	90
4.3	Massive quantitative easing failed to increase credit to private sector	92
4.4	Drastic liquidity injection failed to increase Japan's money supply	93
4.5	Except for three occasions, bankers were willing to lend, but borrowers refused to borrow	95
4.6	Japan: GDP growth despite massive loss of wealth and private-sector deleveraging	97
4.7	Monetary easing is not a substitute for fiscal stimulus (I)	99
4.8	Monetary easing is not a substitute for fiscal stimulus (II)	100
4.9	Japan: Premature Fiscal Reforms in 1997 and 2001	102
4.10	Micro and macro factors behind the Greek-German competitiveness gap	112

4.11 Germany: balance sheet recession after the
1999–2000 telecom bubble 114

4.12 German households stopped borrowing money
after IT bubble 114

4.13 Germany: post telecom-bubble recovery led by
exports to the Euro zone 117

4.14 Expected convergence of unit labor costs in the
Euro zone 119

4.15 The exit problem: the United States took 30 years
to normalize interest rates after 1929 because of
private-sector aversion to debt 125

5.1 Industrialized countries and emerging market
economies: quarterly GDP growth, 2007–2012 136

5.2 Industrialized countries and emerging market
economies: change in export volume of goods and
services, 2006–2012 137

Table

4.1 Industrialized countries and emerging market
economies: quarterly GDP growth, 2007-2012 130

Preface

This book takes up economic issues that concern a large number of countries and are likely to affect all of us in one way or another. It also shows ways that could lead out of the current crisis. The alternative economic policies lined out here are likely to be more effective than the measures taken in the past few years, because they come from an understanding of the underlying problems, which is not based on simplistic theories but on recognition of how the complex economic system functions in reality.

The incomes of a majority of the population have been stagnating, or even falling, in a large number of countries for several years now. At the same time a few people have become outrageously rich. In many countries, large sections of the population, and in particular the youth, are threatened by joblessness. No doubt, the shock of the big financial crisis caused many politicians and decision-makers to have second thoughts about the functioning of the financial system. But too many have returned too soon to resume "business as usual." Today, many defend the same erroneous doctrines that have led us into the crisis, and often they do this even more vigorously than before.

The consequences of the crisis can be discussed by looking at its impact on everyday life and on the actual living conditions of the ordinary people. One may also criticize policymakers and lament about how little of what is possible is actually done by those who have political power. This is not what is intended with this book. Rather, the idea was to bring together economists with different analytical approaches, and from different parts of world, to discuss a few key issues: Why does the world economy time and again undergo deep crises? Why is the financial system so difficult to control? Why have we failed to defeat hunger, hardship, and joblessness in this world of affluence?

It was clear from the outset that the task could not simply be to denounce incapable politicians. A famous economist stated decades ago that "practical men, who believe themselves to be quite exempt from any intellectual influence, are usually the slaves of some defunct economist" and that the difficulty lies not so much in developing new ideas as in escaping from old ones. Each of the five contributions to this volume offers a different perspective on this problem.

Paul Davidson, one of today's leading experts and proponents of Keynesianism, takes up the key question of what we know about the course of history. This question is essential because a large part of the economic profession is operating with models based on a deterministic worldview. This "mainstream" supposes that the course of history cannot be altered and that the scope for actively influencing macroeconomic outcomes is extremely limited. Against this, Davidson presents a more realistic worldview in which there is considerable scope to shape the economic future. If decision-makers are willing to learn from experience, they can fundamentally modify people's living conditions.

James K. Galbraith, one of the most prominent critics of US and European mainstream economics, outlines the course of economic thinking and its errors over the past 80 years. In particular, he shows the failures of economic policymaking in recent decades, from the oil crises in the 1970s to the big crisis of 2008. He suggests entirely new thinking about economic processes, which he considers indispensable for a turnaround.

Richard Koo, arguably the best-known expert on the Japanese economy and on the consequences of financial crises, argues that the present crisis can only be overcome on the basis of a macroeconomic reasoning that takes into account the interdependence of the entire system. He shows that in many countries proactive government policies, especially fiscal policies, are indispensable. It will be essential, in particular, to remove the taboo regarding government indebtedness, because in situations as at present public borrowing is a necessary counterpart to private saving.

Jayati Gosh, the renowned Indian economist and expert for development policies, explains why policy recommendations for developing countries and emerging market economies must take into account also the challenges of their integration into the world economy and their specific structural and institutional features, notwithstanding the fact that the intellectual underpinnings of orthodox policies in the South have been the same as in the North.

Heiner Flassbeck, one of the most prominent critical voices among German economists and an influential financial market expert, shows that both financial and labor markets are functioning in a manner that is very different from what the economic mainstream supposes. Once a crisis like the present one has generated higher unemployment, there is no simple market mechanism assuring a return to full employment through lower wages. In the absence of such a mechanism, however, the intellectual edifice on which economic policies are based becomes extremely shaky.

In the "manifesto" concluding this book, these economists jointly call for a fundamental turnaround in economic thinking and policymaking. In their view, a successful restoration of the market economy crucially depends on throwing the old doctrines overboard. They urge immediate policy action, building on the new insights. Otherwise, not only the economic order, but also the political order will be endangered in many countries. And at the global level, economic and financial integration can only function when it is accompanied by an effective global system of rules.

The experience of the 1920s must be taken as a warning: back then, there was a belief that the less capitalism is restricted the better it will function. This was clearly wrong, and several generations had to suffer the consequences of this misguided proposition. Today, there is trouble ahead again. Five years after the great financial crisis the way back to normalcy—with economic growth driven by rising incomes of the majority of the population—still remains to be found. But it is not yet too late to change course. Fiscal austerity, wage compression, and letting the financial system operate with a minimum of restriction, combined with the pursuit of—allegedly—national interests at the expense of other countries cannot be considered appropriate responses to the big challenges of our time.

CHAPTER 1

Uncertainty and Austerity Policy

Paul Davidson

Decision-Making in Economics

The economy is a process in historical time. Time is a device that prevents everything from happening at once. The production of commodities takes time; and the consumption of goods, especially durables, takes considerable time. Economics is primarily the study of how households and firms make decisions regarding production and consumption activities that have an outcome (payoff) occurring at some time in the future.

Any explanation of the behavior of economic decision-makers, therefore, requires the analyst to make some assumptions regarding (a) what decision-makers expect to be the future outcome of any decision they make today; and (b) whether those expectations will be met. This is most obvious in decisions about investment in plant and equipment, where the realized rate of return will be achieved, and therefore known, only years after the decision to invest is made. Once the decision is made, the decision-maker is stuck with the investment over its useful life. Investment in plant and equipment is like marriage in a conservative society—investor and investment united "till death do them part."

Will the rate of return actually made over the life of the investment be the same as that the entrepreneur anticipated at the moment the investment decision was made? And how did the entrepreneur initially arrive at his/her expected future return?

A majority of economists assume that uncertainty about the future can be measured by an objective probability distribution that can be identified today from existing market data. These analysts are essentially assuming that investors have "rational expectations" and therefore the ability to know the future with actuarial accuracy.[1] This ability is the basis of the theory of efficient capital markets, for, if the future is reliably statistically predictable, then investor participants in today's markets "know" what the future payout of any investment will be. Accordingly, in their self-interest, investors will allocate scarce capital to those investments that are "known" to provide the largest rates of return among all possible alternative investment projects. Investments made by self-interested investors who "know" future returns, therefore, will produce socially optimal returns for the community. It therefore follows that if government interferes in any way with individual decisions in the operation of these free markets, the result will be a less efficient outcome. Consequently, the basic policy view of those who connect uncertainty with the measurement of a probability distribution calculated from existing data on market fundamentals is one of laissez-faire, that is, government should never regulate or otherwise interfere in market operations.

For decisions made today regarding the purchase of financial assets, it is also true that the realized rate of return over the life of the financial asset will only be known ex post, that is, at the end of the financial asset's life. Again, we may ask if the realized return will be equal to what was expected at the time when the purchase decision was made. The answer is: if uncertainty is measured by a known objective probability distribution, then the market expectation of return at the moment of purchase of the financial asset will be validated by the realized rate of return over the life of the asset.

If, however, the financial asset is liquid, that is, traded in a well-organized and orderly liquid market,[2] then the moment the asset holder decides something unexpected is going wrong, he/she can make a *fast exit* by quickly selling the asset in the market. In other words, if, as the future unfolds, something unexpected occurs that makes the investor fear he/she made a mistake, a liquid asset can be quickly sold for money at a price close to the last transaction's market price, thereby limiting the possibility of a lower return or even significant loss if the asset remained in the investor's portfolio. Consequently, in the case of liquid assets, the cojoining of investor and liquid asset is like marriage in a society where divorce is readily available.

The idea expressed here that suddenly "something unexpected occurs" is only meaningful if the future is uncertain in the sense that it cannot be reliably predicted by any statistical analysis of existing market data at the moment the decision on purchasing the financial asset is being taken. If, however, the financial asset is illiquid, that is, nonnegotiable, then the holder is stuck with the asset "until death do them part," even if something unexpected occurs.

In contrast to the idea that the future is knowable by calculating a probability distribution from existing market data, in the analytical framework of John Maynard Keynes (1936) the future is uncertain in the sense that it is not knowable today. Accordingly, the decision to invest in plant and equipment "can only be taken as a result of [the investor-entrepreneur's] animal spirits...and not as the outcome of a weighted average of quantitative benefits multiplied by quantitative probabilities" (161). The existence of organized liquid financial "markets wherein...assets can be easily realised [sic] for money" (161) only makes good sense for those individuals who have some wealth to invest but "the alternative of purchasing actual capital assets cannot be rendered sufficiently attractive (especially to the man who does not manage the capital assets and knows very little about them)" (160–61).

Accordingly, economists are split into two major theoretical camps vis-à-vis the meaning of uncertainty regarding possible knowledge of future outcomes—namely, orthodox mainstream economists, on the one hand, and Keynesian/Post-Keynesian economists, on the other. Each of these camps provides a different explanation of macroeconomic problems and the role of government policy in resolving them. Recognizing the differences between these two concepts of uncertainty is essential to understanding the philosophical differences between economists who espouse a laissez-faire, free-market philosophy and those who argue there is an important role for active government policy to remedy, or at least reduce, the anguish caused by continually upcropping economic problems.

The assumption that all uncertainty can be reduced to a known objective probability distribution leads the orthodox mainstream economists to promote the Panglossian[3] belief that free competitive markets always produce socially optimal solutions. The existence of investment bubbles such as the "dot.com" bubble of the 1990s or the housing market bubble in many countries in the early years of the twenty-first century is logically incompatible with the mainstream analysis. The latter presumes that in pursuing their self-interest individual decision-makers can use existing probability distributions to "know" the future. Yet, the global economy suffered a severe financial shock when the bubble in the subprime mortgage financial derivatives market burst in 2007. In a world where the uncertain future can be reliably predicted via probability distribution, how is it possible that free financial markets experience bubbles that wreak havoc on the global economic system when they burst?

In an amazing "mea culpa" testimony before the US Congress on October 23, 2008, former Federal Reserve chairman Alan Greenspan admitted that he had overestimated the ability of free financial markets to efficiently allocate funds in a socially optimal way, and that he had entirely missed the possibility that financial market deregulation could unleash such a destructive force on the economy as occurred in 2007–2008. In his testimony Greenspan stated: "I still do not fully understand why it happened, and obviously to the extent that I figure it happened and why, I shall change my views."[4]

Like Greenspan, his successor at the Fed, Ben Bernanke, and most mainstream economists have explained the 2007–2008 collapse of the investment banks and the shadow banking system by a "mispricing of [probabilistic] risk" regarding future outcomes. If, however, a reliable statistical calculation of the probability distribution that governs financial and investment markets is made, it would seem impossible to "misprice" the calculated probabilistic risk.

Yet, the major investment bankers were utilizing complex probabilistic "risk management" pricing computer models based on the analysis developed by Nobel Prize winning economists (as Greenspan noted in his testimony). These models continued to attract investment bankers despite the fact that Nobel laureate Myron Scholes's capital asset pricing model had contributed to the collapse, in the late 1990s, of the hedge fund Long Term Capital Management, of which Scholes himself was a director. The "quants" on Wall Street just said we have to develop better models, that is, more sophisticated statistical computer models, to better manage risk! Even today, the mainstream solution to the financial crisis is to let bankers develop even better risk management models, which—if one believes, as Keynes did, that uncertainty about the future cannot be measured in terms of probabilities—may result in yet another financial collapse.

Those who believe in the rational expectations hypothesis would at best admit that disruptive events such as the burst of a speculative bubble are merely short-run exogenous disturbances. They would claim that in the long run, if our faith in laissez-faire is maintained, the economies of all nations will experience global full employment prosperity. Keynes (1936: 192) noted that such a claim of mainstream theorists "offers us the supreme intellectual achievement...of adopting a hypothetical world remote from experience as though it were the world of experience and then living in it consistently."

In this chapter we will explain to Greenspan and others who adopt this hypothetical world to support their Panglossian belief that free markets produce socially optimal solutions why they are wrong, and how Keynes's concept of uncertainty leads to the conclusion that laissez-faire markets cannot be efficient.

Knowing the Future

Ricardo (1817) and his classical followers in the nineteenth century postulated a world of perfect certainty. All households and businesses were assumed to possess a full and correct knowledge of a preprogrammed external economic reality that governed all past, present, and future economic outcomes. The external future economic environment was assumed immutable in the sense that it was not susceptible to change induced by human action. The path of the economy, like the path of the planets under Newton's celestial mechanics, was determined by timeless natural laws. Since economic decision-makers were presumed to have complete knowledge of these laws, households and firms would never make errors in their spending choices. They would spend all their income on things with the highest-"known" future payoff in terms of utility for households and profit for businesses. Accordingly, there could never be a lack of demand for the products of industry or for workers who wanted to work.

The presumed complete knowledge of the future by all decision-makers in a Ricardian classical model justified a laissez-faire philosophy for the economic system. No government action could provide a higher payoff than the decisions that perfectly informed, self-interested individuals made about the future in free markets.

By the end of the nineteenth century economists were trying to introduce some concept of uncertainty into the Ricardian framework. In an economic world where nothing is certain, how can decision-makers "know" the future economic payoff of any decision made today? In response to such questions, early-twentieth-century classical economists tended to replace the perfect knowledge assumption of earlier classical theory by the notion of probabilistic risk premiums and "certainty equivalents" to claim actuarial certainty.

By the 1970s this classical risk analysis had evolved into what economists call the New Classical Theory of "rational expectations," where individuals make decisions based on their subjective probability distributions that are presumed to be equal to immutable objective probability distributions. Today's orthodox economists interpret uncertainty in economics as synonymous with objective probability distributions (Lucas and Sargent, 1981; Machina, 1987) that govern future events. It is presumed that all persons today are able to draw a sample from existing data and to calculate from that data the statistical probabilities of any future outcome.

This device of presuming the use of statistically determined reliable probabilistic risks for measuring uncertainty permits orthodox economists to preserve intact most of the philosophical conclusions that had been developed by Ricardo and his followers. While rejecting Ricardo's perfect certainty model, today's mainstream economists still accept, as a universal truth, the existence of a predetermined economic reality (similar to Newton's celestial mechanics), a reality that can be accurately described by unchanging objective conditional probability functions, which are fully known by the decision-makers. The assumption that people with rational expectations already "know" the objective probabilities assures correct choices on average for those "fittest" decision-makers who survive in the Darwinian world of free markets.

Keynes (1936: 3) stated that the fundamental postulates underlying classical economic theory where the future is knowable "are applicable to a special case only and not to the general case ... [The] characteristics of the special case assumed by the classical theory happen not to be those of the economic society in which we actually live, with the result that its teaching is misleading and disastrous if we attempt to apply it to the facts of experience." The presumption that uncertainty about the future can be reduced to a probabilistic risk measured by an existing probability distribution is a "special case" supported by a fundamental axiom that is not applicable to the world of experience. Keynes's warning about the teaching of such a "special case" is equally applicable to the advice given by mainstream economists to policymakers today, for example, the economic austerity discussions in Washington, the United Kingdom, the Euro zone, China, and elsewhere.

Uncertainty and the Ergodic Axiom

In mainstream economics, market data are typically viewed as being generated by something statisticians call an "ergodic" stochastic process. In fact, Nobel Prize winner Paul Samuelson (1969) has made the acceptance of the ergodic axiom of statistical theory the sine qua non of the scientific method in economics.

The dictionary defines an "axiom" as a statement the analyst believes is a "universal truth" that does not have to be proved. What is this universal truth of ergodicity that Samuelson claims is necessary to make economics a science?

Logically, to draw any statistical (risk) inferences regarding any universe of possible observations, one should draw a sample from that universe and analyze the probability distribution associated with that sample. Accordingly, to make statistically reliable probability forecasts of future economic outcomes, one should draw and analyze a sample from the future market universe. Since drawing a sample from the future is impossible, the ergodic axiom assumes that the future is already predetermined and that a sample from the past is equivalent to one from the future.

In other words, the presumption that future economic outcomes are the result of ergodic stochastic economic processes is
what permits the analyst to assert, without proof, that drawing a
sample from existing past and current market data is equivalent
to drawing a sample from the future universe of market data.
Consequently, what is being presumed is that the probabilistic
outcome at any future date is already bundled in the existing market data, that is, the future is merely the statistical shadow of past
and current market data.

When it is assumed that decision-makers in one's economic
analysis possess rational expectations, then self-interested decision-makers will have processed information embedded in past
and present existing market data to form statistical averages (or
decision weights) that reliably forecast the future. Or, as Thomas
Sargent (1993: 3), one of the leaders of the rational expectations
school, states: "Rational expectations models impute much more
knowledge to the agents within the model (who use the equilibrium probability distributions)...than is possessed by an econo-
metrician, who faces estimation and inference problems that the
agents in the model have somehow solved."

In the twentieth century, however, there were also some economists who questioned the wisdom of using probabilistic risks as a
measure of uncertainty. Beginning with Knight's (1921) seminal
work, a distinction between "true" uncertainty and probabilistic risk was drawn, where the latter is calculable based on past
frequency distributions and is, therefore, conceptually insurable,
while "true" uncertainty is neither calculable nor insurable.

In his *General Theory* (1936), Keynes launched a revolution
in economics by emphasizing that uncertainty in economics is
different from probabilistic risk. He argued that the difference

between probabilistic risk and uncertainty had important implications for understanding (a) the operations of a market (money-
using economy); and (b) the role of government in influencing
market outcomes through deliberate legislative policies.

Unlike today's mainstream economists, Keynes did not write
in the idiom of stochastic processes in developing his concept of
uncertainty since the theory of ergodic stochastic systems was
developed by the Moscow mathematical school of probability in
1935 and was not recognized in the West until after World War
II and Keynes was dead. Keynes (1937) simply described uncertainty as occurring when there is no scientific basis to form any
calculable probability.

With the development of ergodic statistical theory it has
become possible to interpret Keynes's uncertainty concept in
terms of this statistical lexicon.[5] Keynes's theory required decision-makers to recognize that, in the market system in which
they operate, the future is uncertain and cannot be reliably predicted on the basis of any statistical analysis of past evidence.
In a nonergodic environment, even if agents have the capacity
to obtain and statistically process past and current market data,
these observations do not, and cannot, provide a statistically reliable basis for forecasting the probability distributions that will
govern outcomes at any specific date in the future: "About these
[future] matters there is no scientific basis to form any calculable
probability whatever. We simply do not know" (Keynes, 1937:
137). Thus, Keynes was, in essence, arguing that economics was
a nonergodic science.

Keynes's uncertainty concept implies that the future is trans-
mutable or creative in the sense that future economic outcomes
may be permanently changed in nature and substance by today's

actions of individuals, groups (e.g., unions, cartels), and/or governments, often in ways not even perceived by the creators of such change. (Changes that are not predetermined can occur even without any deliberate human economic action.)

This nonergodic view of modeling uncertainty has been described by Nobel Prize winner Sir John Hicks (1977: vii) as a situation where people in the model "do not know what is going to happen and know that they do not know what is going to happen. As in history!"

Why does accepting the ergodic axiom by mainstream economists make a difference in determining the role of government in the economy? Samuelson, Lucas, and other mainstream, orthodox economists have adopted, either explicitly or implicitly, the ergodic axiom because they want economics to be in the same class as the "hard sciences" such as astronomy. The science of astronomy is based on the presumption of an ergodic stochastic process that governs the movement of all the heavenly bodies from the moment of the "Big Bang" to the day the universe ends. Accordingly, statistical analyses using past measurements of the movements of heavenly bodies permit astronomers to predict future solar eclipses within a few seconds of when they actually occur.

Indeed, nothing that the US Congress, the president of the United States, the United Nations, or environmentalists can do will alter the predetermined dates and time for future solar eclipses. For example, Congress cannot pass enforceable legislation outlawing solar eclipses in order to provide more sunshine and thereby enhance crop production. In an ergodic world, all future events are predetermined and beyond change by human action today.

By contrast, in a nonergodic world human actions can shape the future. This has consequences for the role of government policies in the economy. If one asserts that economics is an ergodic process, then there is no role for government to alter the already predetermined future. Government must adopt a laissez-faire philosophy toward economic matters if economics, like astronomy, is an ergodic science! If, however, economics is a nonergodic science, then proper government policies can create the economic future to improve the human standard of living relative to what would occur under a laissez-faire system of government.

Austerity as a Solution to Debt

In the world of experience, people know they do not know the future. How can households and enterprises, therefore, protect themselves from possible adverse circumstances affecting their income, standard of living, and livelihood?

Our modern capitalist society has attempted to create an arrangement that will provide people with some, albeit far from complete, control over their uncertain economic future. In capitalist economies, money and legally binding money contracts are used to organize production and the sales and purchases of all goods and services in the marketplace. This system of money contracting permits individual households and enterprises to have a degree of control over their future cash inflows and outflows and therefore control over their monetary income and outlays for the economic future.

For example, households enter into money contracts where they agree to pay rent or to make mortgage loan payments on their homes; they also sign contracts to make payments to electric, gas, and telephone utility companies for their providing services over time. These contracts give households cost control over major aspects of their cost of living today and for months and perhaps years to come. They also provide the other parties (business firms) to these money contracts with the legal promise of current and future cash inflows sufficient to meet the business firms' current and expected future money costs of production and to generate a profit for providing the agreed goods and/or services. Money wage contracts provide business firms control over their current and future labor costs of production; they also provide employees control over their current and future money incomes.

People and business firms willingly enter into money contracts because each party thinks it is in their best interest to fulfil the terms of the contractual agreement. By entering into contractual arrangements people assure themselves a measure of predictability in terms of their contractual cash inflows and outflows, even in a world of uncertainty.

For decisions that involve potential large cash outflows, people "know" that they cannot predict what the future will hold. They do know, however, that for these decisions involving expensive cash outflows, making a mistake with regard to assumptions about the future can be very costly. Consequently, decision-makers believe that saving a portion of their current income, rather than spending it entirely, maybe a judicious decision.

If people do not spend their entire current income on newly produced goods and services, they save part of it in some form of liquid assets. This saving is seen as a protection against some unforeseen adverse occurrence in the saver's working life and/or for providing purchasing power in retirement. Any portion of a current income that is currently not spent on the products of industry (i.e., saved) means a lower market demand for goods and services, and therefore less profit opportunities for business firms compared to a situation in which decision-makers spend their entire income on today's products of industry.

The portion of income that is saved will be spent to purchase liquid assets, that is, financial assets that can readily be resold for money in case money is needed to discharge a future contractual obligation that may arise even if it is unforeseen currently. Liquid assets are essentially "time machines" that permit their holder to park potential contractual settlement purchasing power and move this power into the indefinite future. These liquid asset time machines are not produced by labor (as producible goods and services are), so spending part of one's current income on the purchase of these liquidity time machines does not create a current demand for labor that produces goods and services. Accordingly, current market demand for labor to produce goods and services is always diminished by savings relative to the market demand that would exist if all the income of savers was spent on the products of industry.

For the market demand for goods and services to remain high and therefore maintain high employment when there is positive aggregate savings in the community, there must be other decision-makers who wish to spend more than their current income on goods and services, thereby creating jobs to offset the loss of jobs created by savers. These more-than-current-income spenders obtain the extra spending money by borrowing, that is, going into debt.

Who are these other decision-makers, who are willing to go into debt and thereby offset the aggregate propensity of the savers to save in each calendar period? Economists believe (hope?) that it will be private entrepreneurs who are willing to borrow to purchase new plant and equipment, relying on their "animal spirits."

These "animal spirits" must be such that the entrepreneurs expect new investments to be productive and to generate an additional cash inflow that is sufficiently high to allow the firm to pay all its operating costs and make a profit besides servicing the annual debt payment and paying off the principal amount of the debt over the life of the new equipment. Borrowing by investors to purchase new plant and equipment, although desirable, may not always be attainable in a world of uncertainty, unless entrepreneurs have sufficient "animal spirits" so they are confident their dreams of the profitability of new investment will come true.

Suppose private investors do not see their way to deficit spend on new plant and equipment to such an extent as would be necessary to maintain employment at close to the full employment level. Are there other decision-makers who are willing to go into debt to maintain the nation's high level of employment?

If the government decides to spend more, then this deficit spending on socially useful products such as infrastructure and other facilities to benefit its citizens will create jobs. One of the responsibilities of government is to assure prosperity by doing all that it can to make certain there are sufficient profit opportunities for the nation's industries and job opportunities for its residents. Accordingly, government deficit spending on the products of industry to stimulate the economy to maintain or obtain full employment should occur whenever planned savings out of private-sector income exceed what private investors are willing to borrow in connection with investment in new productive plant and equipment (see also the contribution of Richard Koo to this volume).[6] (On the other hand, if total private-sector spending is already sufficient to maintain full employment, then government deficit spending is neither necessary nor desirable.)

In the real world, when unemployment is high or rising, households recognize that the future is more uncertain and will try to reduce their cash outflows merely as a precautionary device to protect themselves from possible economic misfortune. If, however, the government stimulus plan actually offers more profitable money contracts to enterprises to produce goods and services, then, armed with these money contractual commitments that assure cash inflows, firms will expand production and hire more workers without fear of the uncertain future.

In order to understand the role of debt spending as a means of creating jobs and income one must recognize the double-entry bookkeeping accounting fact that for every saver there must be a borrower. Accordingly, if private-sector actors (households and most business firms) in the aggregate desire to save by reducing their purchases of goods and services out of current income, then either other investors or the government must deficit-spend in order to maintain output and employment and validate the increase in savings desired by households and firms.

In an open global economy, the nation can hope for its trading partners to go into debt to purchase more exports from the nation than its own residents spend on imports. In other words, an export surplus for any nation with otherwise unemployed labor and capital equipment is a stimulus for income and prosperity for the nation's inhabitants. Unfortunately, however, not all nations can simultaneously obtain export surpluses (see also the chapter by Heiner Flassbeck in this volume).

Solution for "Overextended" Debtors

At some point of time, the savers may question the ability of debtors—individual borrowers or governments—to continue to service their existing debt, and even more their ability to increase their debt obligations in the future. Debtors may be perceived as having overextended themselves in debt obligations. Consequently, the savers will not willingly provide their savings to purchase in the market new additional debt contracts being offered by the perceived-to-be-overextended debtors.

If the overextended debtor is a household, conventional wisdom leads the debtor household to go on an austerity program, that is, to reduce its spending on goods and services out of current income significantly and to use the saved cash flow (from the assumed unchanged income) to service and reduce its debt. Of course, when the household undertakes such an austerity program, it tends to reduce the sales and income of those firms who had counted on the debtor household as a customer. The income reduction for these firms and their employees is, however, small in the aggregate and therefore is unlikely to have repercussions on the level of income of the household debtor who raised its savings in the first instance.

There is, however, an alternative to austerity for this household debtor: If the household has some unemployed resources, it could use these idle resources to engage in additional economic activity to increase its total household income.[7] The additional income earned can then be used to service the existing outstanding debt without reducing the household's current purchases of goods and services. This is a win-win situation for all concerned.

When a government is considered to be an "overextended" debtor, conventional wisdom is to apply the same economic austerity approach as one uses for an individual household debtor, that is, to require the government to engage in an austerity fiscal program of reducing its expenditure and possibly increasing taxes to try to run a fiscal surplus, or at least a balanced budget. However, this has quite different implications for the economy and the debtor. A government fiscal budget is so large relative to the national economy that the government's cutting back its spending on goods and services and/or increasing income tax rates will create significant unemployment in the production sectors whose goods would otherwise have been purchased by the government and/or those who are now subject to higher tax rates. The outcome will be to significantly lower the total income in these sectors of the economy.

The resulting fall in the income of the affected private sectors will induce a further decline in private spending on goods and services. The result will be a vicious cycle of increased unemployment and reduced profits for enterprises. This will ultimately reduce the government's tax revenues. Therefore, an austerity program imposed on a nation whose government is deemed overextended in debt is not likely to achieve its goal of reducing the government's debt obligations. It will serve primarily to reduce the income and employment of its residents.[8]

Austerity for a nation carries the threat of higher unemployment and even a lower ability to service its outstanding debt obligations. Only if the residents of the nation experience an increase in income can the government expect a rise in tax revenue to help service its outstanding debt.

In an open global economy, there is often an imbalance among trading partners between the value of exports and the value of imports in a calendar period. A nation with an export surplus can be conceived as spending less than the income it has generated by its exports with the products of its trading partners. In other words, the nation is saving part of its income from international trade, and these trade surplus savings will be embodied in the liquid asset known as foreign reserves accruing to the nation.

If one nation has a trade surplus, then one or more of its trading partners must have a trade deficit, which is financed either by loans from the surplus nation or by a selling off of its liquid foreign reserves. Obviously, if this situation persists, sooner or later the deficit nation will run out of reserves, and/or lenders in the surplus nation will refuse to finance the deficit nation's excess of imports over its exports. Any attempt to impose austerity on the trade deficit nation, if successful, will adversely affect the sale of exports of the surplus nation. The result can be a collapse of global income and trade.

The preferable solution, as the Keynes Plan presented at Bretton Woods indicated, is to create a mechanism that induces the trade surplus nation(s) to spend more on export goods and services produced by the trade deficit nation(s). As long as the debtor nation(s) have unemployed resources, this creates additional income in the deficit nation(s), and thereby permits a debtor nation to work its debt down and thereby remove any global recessionary forces. This is a win-win result for the global economy.

Notes

1. That is, with the same degree of accuracy as can be obtained by using methods that are applied in the insurance industry for calculating insurance risks and premiums.

2. The institutions necessary to ensure a well-organized and orderly market are discussed in my book, *The Keynes Solution: The Path to Global Economic Prosperity* (New York and London: Palgrave/Macmillan, 2009).

3. "Panglossian" is the view that all is for the best in this best of possible worlds.

4. Greenspan also stated: "This crisis, however, has turned out to be much broader than anything I could have imagined...In recent decades, a vast risk management and pricing system has evolved, combining the best insights of mathematicians and finance experts supported by major advances in computer and communications technology. A Nobel Prize was awarded for the discovery of the [free-market] pricing model that underpins much of the advance in [financial] derivatives markets. This modern risk management paradigm held sway for decades. The whole intellectual edifice, however, collapsed."

5. In criticizing Tinbergen's use of econometric analysis, Keynes (1939) argued that Tinbergen's method was not applicable to economic data because "the economic environment is not homogenous over a period of time." This criticism is equivalent to stating that economic time series are not stationary, and nonstationarity is a sufficient condition for nonergodicity.

6. Those who do not want government to deficit spend under any circumstance often invoke the so-called Ricardian equivalence effect. The advocates of Ricardian equivalence argue that households know with certainty their future tax liabilities. They "know," it is asserted, that today's deficit spending will require the government to raise tax rates in the future in order to obtain the higher tax revenues that are required for the repayment of this additional debt. It follows that these all-knowing households will immediately match the increase in government spending with additional savings to prepare to pay the additional forthcoming taxes. In other words, Ricardian equivalence advocates assert, without proof, that any increase in government spending will be immediately matched by a decrease in private-sector spending on goods and services.

Of course, if the future is very uncertain (as it is currently in the Euro zone), then households are putting as much of their current income as possible into savings. These savings are used to buy liquid assets (perhaps even US-dollar-denominated assets). Accordingly, if a government in the Euro zone initiates a stimulus program to create additional market demand and jobs, believers in the Ricardian equivalence effect argue that there would be no additional market demand and jobs created. Why? Tax payers would increase their savings out of current income to pay the expected future higher taxes necessary to service the deficit-financed stimulus program. In other words, the Ricardian equivalence effect induces an increase in current tax payer savings that results in lowering market demand for goods and services just as the stimulus policy increases market demand for goods and services. The net effect is no gain in market demand and jobs. The Ricardian equivalence is obviously false, naïve, and foolish in a world of nonergodic uncertainty.

7. The unemployed resources could be a second income earner in the household or idle time of the primary income earner of the household, which allows him or her to take on a second job or other income earning activity.

8. Some argue that this increase in the debtor nation's unemployment is good in the sense that will reduce workers' wage rates (directly and/or via currency devaluation) and therefore make the debtor nation's export industries "more competitive" in world markets. Unfortunately, unless there is somehow an increase in global aggregate demand, these "more competitive" industries just mean that unemployment is exported to other nations.

CHAPTER 2

New Thinking and a Strategic Policy Agenda

James K. Galbraith

A Crisis in Ideas

It has been rightly stated that the financial crisis of 2008 exposed a deep flaw in the way economics had approached the problems of prosperity, marketplace stability, and growth. The widely accepted conventional view before the crisis held that the ideal policy would impose minimal frictions and interventions, leaving markets to establish and maintain "equilibrium" relationships between all players, with each receiving a return proportionate to their contribution. This applied in national policies to the preference for privatization, deregulation, and flat taxes, and internationally to a preference for free trade, free capital flows, and continental economic unions. In finance, the "efficient-markets hypothesis" held that capital asset prices would reflect the best information available to economic agents—a doctrine implying that major crises were, at best, inherently unpredictable.

Meanwhile technological progress was viewed as the defining feature of the age, bringing economic development and better living standards everywhere. Rising economic inequality was considered largely to reflect the requirements of new technologies and therefore was, at best, a secondary concern. Indeed, the losers from the technological revolution were presumed to be few, and their problems open to solution with education and training programs. Innovation was also greatly celebrated in finance, notably for its supposed ability to dissipate risk.

In this world, it was thought that labor market and wage flexibility would assure efficiency and, especially, foster full employment. Greater educational opportunity and training programs could help control inequality. Transparency and the desire to maintain reputation were thought sufficient to assure the integrity of market processes. Capital-adequacy requirements would stabilize and protect the banks. Deficit and debt limits and credible inflation-targeting would assure macroeconomic stability and continue the "Great Moderation." In developing countries especially, privatization, deregulation, and the abolition of subsidies would lift the dead hand of the state, assuring undistorted prices, more efficient resource allocation, and more rapid economic growth. Computable general equilibrium models estimated the gains that could be had by aligning prices with those determined in a free market.

These ideas and measures formed a comprehensive body of doctrine and were widely accepted. In the circles of academic economics and the financial press they were largely uncontroversial. It was thought that once they had been fully adopted and implemented, with the resistance from those opposed to progress overcome, public policy would hold few challenges; the major problems had been solved.

The great financial crisis and its aftermath, including the crisis in the Euro zone, reveal every part of this to have been illusion. It is not just that pieces of this worldview—such as the efficient-markets hypothesis—require revision, in view of the vast scale of the debacle and the fortunes made by some who saw what was coming. The entire conceptual scheme and policy framework has fallen down. That which had dominated the teaching and practice of economics for a generation, is gone. And so the question arises, what (if anything) can be put in its place?

Luckily—at least, luckily up to a point—this is not the first time a dominant paradigm collapsed. It is actually, within the span of a century, the *third time* that this happened. Since the collapse of the first such paradigm, in the Great Depression, is well remembered, this chapter will start by revisiting the second, more recent, but comparatively overlooked one.

The Forgotten 1970s and the Resources Problem

The dominant economic narrative of the twentieth century was the collapse of laissez-faire in the Great Depression, and the rise (especially following World War II) of a mixed economy with a strong public sector acting to stabilize aggregate effective demand. In postwar America—and later in Europe and elsewhere—there grew up a synthesis of neoclassical and Keynesian economics, augmented in the 1960s by the theory of the Phillips Curve. Given good management, this offered the promise of full employment, unlimited steady economic growth, and even the conquest of the business cycle, marred only by small amounts of inflation. Fortified with this theory, the 1950s and 1960s were a time when intellectual optimism prevailed, first in academic economics and later in governments that academic economists helped to form.

With the spread of democracy alongside generally good economic outcomes, political leaders and electorates alike embraced the responsibility of government for economic success. A main issue, debated within centrist politics (ranging from Christian Democrat to Social Democrat in European terms, from Eisenhower Republicans to Johnson Democrats in the United States), was how best to balance the roles of the public and private sectors. It was where to draw the line between two essential components of a successful economy, a public sector that would manage and supervise, and a private sector that could be relied on to handle the details. Those arguing that either one or the other could be dispensed with—the positions of Mao and von Mises, so to speak—were relegated to the fringes.

The 1970s delivered a rude shock to this consensus. It did this initially by calling attention to a matter not apparently within the control of industrialized countries: the cost of resources, especially of oil.

When stagflation hit the industrial world, it was, and was viewed as, largely a matter of oil shocks, as in 1973 and again in 1979. And while these did not reflect a world shortage of oil, they did reflect the decline in US production after 1970, the oil-short status of continental Europe and Japan, and thus a loss of control over prices, which migrated from Texas (where the key American price had been managed by the Texas Railroad Commission) to OPEC. So, though the shocks had political roots—the Yom Kippur War and the Iranian Revolution—they also had a foundation in changing geophysical realities and this was well understood at the time.

The "concept" of a supply shock threw a wrench into the previously dominant view of demand management. What was the appropriate policy response? Some argued that the rising price of oil was essentially a tax, which could be offset by reducing other taxes or increasing public spending, so as to maintain total employment. In that case, supply controls and incomes policy might be necessary to manage the price effects of the shock. But others saw the shock as simply a vector of inflation, caused by loose money and to be dealt with by tighter money. In that case, the adjustment in terms of lost output and jobs would have to be borne, but (it was argued) that cost would be lower in the long run if faced and taken immediately, preventing inflation from becoming entrenched.

The disagreement continued through several recessions and many variations on anti-inflation policy, until the Thatcher-Reagan revolutions of 1979–1981 settled the argument in favor of the second view. Monetary policy suppressed cost inflation; tax reductions afterward restored purchasing power. This combination of policies put a brutal end to efforts to cope with supply shocks via energy or industrial policies, and also to wage-and-price guidelines or income policies. And this was accompanied by a reinterpretation of the history and economics that put the resource question deep into the background.

The new consensus attributed the unsatisfactory economic performance of the 1970s to mismanagement of monetary policy. This, it argued, was rooted in a flawed conception of the Phillips Curve as a static trade-off between inflation and unemployment. According to this view, inflation stemmed from the misguided pursuit of full employment by central banks, in the face of a "natural rate of unemployment" below which countries were fated to experience accelerating inflation. The correct policy was therefore to target inflation at near-to-zero, allowing the unemployment rate to be set by labor market forces. This was the opposite of the prior worldview, and it triumphed in time to form the foundation of the Maastricht Treaty (restricting the role of expansionary fiscal policy) and the charter of the ECB (committing that institution to price stability above all other objectives).[1] Efforts to improve economic performance would rely on market forces: deregulation, privatization, and the removal of distortions imposed by the tax code.

Just as the experience of the 1960s in the United States appeared to validate the 1960 formulation of the Phillips Curve, so the superior performance of the 1980s and 1990s—in the rich countries—appeared to validate the new consensus. A new term of art, the "Great Moderation," was invented to describe the improvement. And much of the cause was attributed—with very casual causal logic—to the new ideology itself, as implemented by central banks, whose "credibility" was augmented by a new "transparency" and transmitted to the "expectations" of the public. None of the concepts mentioned in quotation marks could, however, be observed.

What was going on outside the insular world of the rich nations, which took the form of debt crises and decades of development lost, was never integrated into this view, except loosely as the price of the prior statist policies ("import-substituting industrialization") now in disfavor. Then in the mid-1980s, commodity prices collapsed, and resource issues receded from memory. Resource costs were therefore never made part of economic thinking—and still have not been. Nevertheless, it is clear that the price of energy today again plays a major role in economic instability, the nonprofitability of private business, and the weak economic growth prospects of the rich oil-consuming countries.

Globalization and the (Provisional) End of Inflation

What really happened in the 1980s? In the consensus view, tough and credible monetary policy achieved disinflation at lower cost than previously expected, bringing on a new golden age of stable economic growth—the Great Moderation. In reality, the pain was intense and the costs were enormous. They fell in part on industrial workers in the wealthy countries, especially in the early 1980s in the United States and the United Kingdom. But they also fell heavily on the rest of the world, on countries dependent on commodity exports or saddled with commercial bank debt.

In the United States an aggressive antilabor policy, collapsed export markets, and high unemployment broke the back of the trade unions and of wage inertia. In the United Kingdom similar policies had similar effects; less so elsewhere in Europe. But the effects of the debt crises of Latin America, Africa, and parts of Asia were more severe. And when world commodity prices collapsed, it was partly under the pressures of a global slump induced by the debt crisis. Then the end of the Soviet Union and its empire opened new resource markets on favorable terms, while the post-Soviet states endured a population implosion. Finally, China emerged as a major supplier of low-cost wage goods to world markets—a reaction in part to the now high cost of production in the advanced countries. These factors, together known as *globalization*, helped to bring 30 years of low inflation to the advanced world.

Disinflation was global. The effects that matter are worldwide effects. It is implausible to focus on the alleged effects of the Federal Reserve's announcement of its monetary targets—an exercise completely unnoticed outside the United States—while ignoring the effects on the prices of consumer goods in world markets brought about by debt-deflation, world recession, industrial collapse in the Soviet Union and Eastern Europe, and the rise of Chinese light industry. Monetary policy in the United States did play a role in these events by increasing the burden of dollar-denominated debts, on the one hand, and by raising the value of the US dollar and opening the US market to imports, on the other. It did not work, as often supposed, in a benign and effortless way by guiding expectations for domestic wage settlements. Low inflation came on condition that world resource demands be held down; if they had continued to rise, the disinflation would have failed.

With the end of inflation, US growth resumed. How? By and large, the decline of industry and trade unions (along with a declining real value of the minimum wage) meant that *wage-led growth* became a thing of the past, both in North America and in Europe. Similarly, *growth led by public investment* disappeared; in the United States infrastructure investment had become dominated by the major states—New York and California contributing large shares—and this ended with the fiscal crisis of New York City in 1975 and the tax revolt in California in 1978. And so in the 1980s and 1990s demand growth in the United States (and other rich countries) came to be driven largely by *credit expansion*. The credit cycle—well-known in the 1920s and 1930s, but largely forgotten after the war—returned. And it chose to favor sectors, beginning with technology and ending with mortgages, that had low variable costs but high fixed costs. This was a critical, little noted adjustment to the now high and uncertain real cost of resources.

The Rise of Finance, Information Technology, and Mortgages

In the one-world, low-inflation economy that emerged from the debt crisis, global financial institutions assumed a dominant role. They did this directly as creditors. They also did it indirectly by imposing a common policy viewpoint—the "Washington Consensus"—on most countries and by rewarding promises of cooperation with loans. At the same time, the levers of financial policy around the world also passed from the hands of professional civil servants to bankers, as seen in the global governmental connections, today, of a handful of major financial firms.

One result is that neoliberal policies were accompanied by rising inequality, in which an increasing income share of the financial sector played an important role. This was most notably true in countries such as Argentina and Brazil where liberalization proceeded most rapidly; but it is a pattern also observed in post-Soviet Russia, and in India and China, as well as in Europe. In the United States financial-sector profits grew to some 40 percent of total profits, and financial-sector wages to around 10 percent of total wages. With increasing wealth came increasing political power, as banks pressed for, and eventually achieved, deregulation of their activities. Major legislative phases were the repeal of the Glass-Steagall Act in 1999 and the Commodity Futures Modernization Act of 2000, forbidding regulation of over-the-counter derivatives. In the 2000s deregulation was followed by "desupervision," as US regulatory authorities made calculated decisions not to investigate financial sector practices.

Within the United States financial markets fueled the information technology boom, producing a period of full employment in the last three years of the twentieth century. The industries so fostered had high fixed and low variable costs—again a predict-able response to the new resource environment. The era of heavy industry in the rich countries was now over. With light demand on resources, there was no increase of inflation. This experience showed that the hypothesis of a "natural rate of unemployment" could not be correct, and so the natural rate was quietly aban-doned by most economists (though it lingered on, unjustifiably, in their models). Full employment was possible so long as global economic activity did not trigger rapidly rising resource prices.

At the same time the flow of incomes and capital-asset valua-tions to the technology sector—located in a tiny geographic region of the United States—accounted for practically all of the increase in income inequality (as observed between counties) in the 1990s. By all measures, income inequality in the United States and in the wider world peaked in the year 2000. When the information technology boom ended, matters began to change. There would not again be a strong expansion based on the flow of credit and of equity investment into businesses, not in the United States or elsewhere.

After the information technology boom ended, a new US admin-istration faced the challenge of restoring and sustaining economic growth under much more difficult conditions. Commodity prices had begun to rise. The attacks of 9/11 added a note of shock and uncertainty to the business climate. Interest rates were cut drasti-cally. So were taxes. And military spending increased, especially when the United States invaded Iraq in March 2003. While these policies stabilized total demand and employment, they could not—and did not—lead the United States back to full employ-ment and threatened to destabilize the cost structure. To sustain economic activity, something more general was needed.

That "something" proved to be a vast increase of mortgage lending, running through 2006 and into early 2007. Mortgages were another high-fixed, low-variable cost industry, fueling activity without imposing major new resource demands. So the strategy worked to raise employment with little effect on inflation, for a time. But this choice had monumental implications for the future of global finance, and so for the future of finance-driven capitalism in North America and also in Europe.

By the end of the 1990s the mortgage market in North America was already mature. It could not therefore grow rapidly on the foundation of previously established standards. Those who met those standards and who wanted mortgages generally had them. The growth rate that could be fueled by expansion of this market was thus limited by population and income growth in the economy at large.

Rapid growth in mortgage lending therefore entailed a decline in underwriting standards. And this could be provoked by sending a clear signal of nonenforcement to mortgage originators.[2] The share of subprime and "alt-a" mortgages—also called "liars' loans"— in total new mortgages increased rapidly. So did the proportion of loans with "teaser rates" and of loans against houses that were appraised for more than their market value. Fraud, abuse, and missing documentation became ubiquitous. To market the bad loans to investors, complex securities were devised and rating agencies were enlisted to certify them as investment-grade. Many of these loans were then sold outside the United States, where investors were willing to trust the reputation of their US counterparties, and unlikely to assess for themselves the quality of the underlying credits.

In this way the expansion of mortgage lending supported growth while imposing only light new demand for resources.

Meanwhile new quantitative techniques were adapted to turn mortgage-backed securities and their derivatives into commodities. These instruments promised high yields with great safety, and the demand for them was very strong. But they were to a very large degree fraudulent; defaults were inevitable and large losses would necessarily fall on the ultimate investor. All of this has been shown by official investigations, including the Financial Crisis Inquiry Commission, the Senate Permanent Committee on Investigations, the Congressional Oversight Panel, and the Special Inspector General for the Troubled Asset Relief Program. The close relationship between mortgage fraud and political power in the United States is perhaps best illustrated by a simple fact: Roland Arnall, the CEO of Ameriquest, one of the most aggressive purveyors of bad mortgages, was able to end his career as ambassador of the United States of America to the Netherlands.

The Doubtful Construction of Europe

Partly in response to the reemerging financial dominance of the United States, a large part of Europe built for itself integrated product and capital markets and a currency union, alongside the previously existing customs union. Labor mobility across countries was made legally easy, though it remained difficult in practice. The European Union and Euro zone fulfilled a long-standing dream of ending the possibility of major European wars and providing a common home for a continent that had been sharply divided by the Cold War.

Yet, this was done on the template of the economic views that were prevailing at the time, which held that policy rules, rather than institutions, would be sufficient to keep the European economy stable and its markets liquid. Institutions (which introduce rigidities) were deprecated as barriers to innovation and employment. Europe would instead unify around a vision of free markets, adopting all the major tenets of neoliberal doctrine, including deregulation, privatization, and cutbacks in the welfare state.

Thus, the European Union adopted the Maastricht criteria for public debt and deficits, the Basel rules for banking, and the inflation-targeting charter of the European Central Bank (ECB). Moreover, Europe denied itself the power, at the continental level, to tax and spends for purposes of economic stabilization and growth, and (at least in principle) it denied its central bank the authority to serve as a formal lender of last resort to member countries. Apart from the lending powers of the European Investment Bank (largely immobilized by matching fund requirements that can no longer be met), Europe lacks fiscal integration and monitoring, automatic stabilizers that work across national frontiers at the EU level, mechanisms to finance public investment, and a common military. It also lacks continental wage standards and programs of social insurance. By contrast, all of these were built into the US system since the 1930s.

Europe thus reinvented the *confederation*—a form of government tested twice and abandoned twice in North America, most recently with the collapse of the Confederate States of America in 1865. It did this just as the resource environment was turning unfavorable for large, integrated, high-fixed-cost social formations. As matters developed, this would make Europe vulnerable to disturbances from the outside, whether they were rooted in resource costs or in finance. Or, as would happen, in both.

The Great Crisis in the United States and Europe

The Great Crisis thus stemmed from the confluence of *three* events in the early 2000s. These were the exhaustion of the information technology boom at the end of the 1990s, the return of higher resource prices, and finally the rise and then the exposure of financial malfeasance, specifically in the market for mortgages, for residential mortgage-backed securities (RMBS), and for derivative instruments based on RMBS in the United States, including Credit Default Swaps.

The collapse of the information technology boom ended a moment of euphoria about American prospects; the exuberant 1990s were replaced by the plodding 2000s. Rising energy prices placed a growing squeeze on profitability in high-fixed-cost, energy-importing countries, while fostering a decade of relative prosperity for the exporters, a prosperity further augmented (post-9/11) by a sharp reduction in interest rates, rapidly growing Chinese demand for commodities, and widespread repudiation of the "Washington Consensus." Energy prices were then accelerated by speculation, peaking in 2008. Meanwhile, as we have seen, growing financial fraud fostered continuing economic growth. But this was necessarily temporary. In Minsky's words, when the Ponzi phase of a credit expansion is exposed, it must end. When the bad quality of US mortgage loans and their derivatives came to light, interbank lending markets froze up, the investment banks headed toward bankruptcy, and the financial sector substantially collapsed.

The American financial shock was then vectored into a vulnerable Europe, owing to the exposure of European financial institutions to US "toxic" assets and to the general rush to liquidity that followed the failure of the interbank lending market in 2007 and of the investment banks in 2008. It is important to grasp the integrated character of these events—which is often obscured by terminology in common use. While each of the countries in the European periphery had undeniable problems, there was no sudden, simultaneous, independent discovery of mismanagement in Greece, commercial real-estate excess in Ireland, a housing bubble in Spain, and so forth. On the contrary, these facts were known to any competent observer. Rather, they were all *facilitated* in the expansion; it is the nature of credit booms that weak borrowers get loans they would not otherwise receive.

In the slump this is reversed, *and* there is overshooting. Where once credit was freely available, now it cannot be had. The precipitating event is not the discovery of new facts; it is the realization that the game is over and that everyone is turning tail. When losses are exposed in one part of a portfolio, the rational reaction is to cut and run from other weak assets. This alone can explain the general and simultaneous flight from all weak Euro zone sovereigns and to the safety of German, British, and US treasury bonds when the scale of the US mortgage debacle became plain.

The crisis that seized Portugal, Ireland, Greece, and Spain, and that continues to threaten Italy and perhaps soon France, was therefore not only a national crisis of these countries. It was at the same time a crisis of the European banking system—highly leveraged and vulnerable to losses. It was a crisis of European institutions, which unlike those in the United States were not created in response to financial crises (in 1907 and 1930) and were poorly designed to cope with systemic stress. And it was a world crisis, reflecting the catastrophic global consequences of financial mismanagement, reckless innovation, and deregulation and the dismantling of supervision of the US banking system. All of this led to a flight to safety, a rejection of risk, and a withdrawal from investment that cost millions of jobs and that continues, after four years, deepening recession in Europe and impeding growth in the United States.

The Reaction and the Aftermath

In the early phase of the crisis, policies focused on returning order and function to financial markets. Yet this proved impossible, since those markets were not merely "illiquid." Actually they had been destroyed in the meltdown. This was true in the United States, where mortgage originators went bankrupt, where investment banks and broker-dealers were acquired by commercial banks, where AIG, Fannie Mae, and Freddie Mac were seized by the government, and where the rating agencies were largely discredited. And it was also true in Europe, where sovereign debt markets continued to exist, but in name only; their previous independence from the implicit guarantee of the European central authorities had vanished. This, however, was harder to acknowledge.

As a fallback, following the Lehman bankruptcy, central banks concentrated on avoiding further failures of major institutions, and on assuring liquidity to the commercial paper market, money market funds, in the financing of dollar liabilities and elsewhere. It was possible to keep large financial institutions alive, in the formal sense, by such measures. Indeed, they were able to offload losses onto the public sector, to dispose of bad assets with the central bank, and to gradually restore their earnings with interest-rate arbitrage and proprietary trading. What they did not and will not do is to return substantially to the old-fashioned and ordinary business of taking commercial and industrial risk and underwriting business investment. That is an activity requiring a very different sort of banking sector than the one that exists presently—or can exist in a resource-constrained world—in the presence of bank behemoths intent on fast profits and on maintaining very high (reported) rates of return.

In Europe, investors sold off the debts of small and peripheral sovereigns, or bought Credit Default Swaps on the same, while the media exposed policy and governance problems in those countries. Policymakers again talked about "restoring confidence" and about taking measures that would return troubled debtors to the credit markets. But these hopes would be dashed over time. Only a worldwide systemic solution to the slump and panic could bring creditors back to a reformed Spain or Ireland—let alone Greece. Of course, such a miracle would not happen. The beleaguered peripheral countries cut their budgets, raised taxes, and attempted such policy reforms as they could manage under highly stressful conditions. But it would never be enough. The simple reason is that the motivation of international investors was governed by another factor entirely, namely, the overpowering urge for "safety first."

On the fiscal front, large automatic stabilizers were supplemented at first by "stimulus" programs. But forecasters followed their normal practice of predicting an early recovery, and these predictions were reflected in official budget documents and thus became the basis of response plans. Stimulus proposals therefore presumed that the downturn was only temporary and that there would in any event be a full recovery once programs to "kick-start" it got under way. This proved to be a major error. Stimulus programs were too small, they ended too soon, and when they failed to achieve the forecast results, they could be (and were) derided as ineffective.

As these events unfolded, ideas were again very slow to change. Some commenters continued to use optimistic forecasts as a benchmark, concluding (since the realized growth was below forecasts) that quantitative easing, fiscal stimulus, and other interventions had retarded a recovery that would otherwise have been faster. This argument helped to fuel a revival of noninterventionist policy ideas.

Now in Europe and in some of the international agencies (including the ECB) the doctrine of "expansionary fiscal consolidation" or "expansionary austerity" came into fashion. This notion held that public spending cuts would actually increase economic activity, through favorable effects on confidence and business expectations of profitability. Examples ranging from Canada and Australia to Latvia have been cited—but none without a rapidly growing trading partner and a strong base in natural resources. Efforts to apply the doctrine of expansionary austerity in the United Kingdom—or any other large economy—are not turning out well. In April 2012, the BBC reported that the United Kingdom had officially entered a "double-dip" recession. In Spain, the unemployment rate has reached 25 percent.

Thus, in Europe matters spiraled toward the controlled default of Greece, which has occurred; ultimately an impending panic was forestalled only by the pledge of the ECB to buy unlimited quantities of Italian and Spanish bonds, if necessary. Meanwhile the US economy moved to an apparently stable state of slow growth and very slowly declining unemployment, but this was largely due to very large continuing fiscal stabilization, to decisions by working Americans to withdraw from the labor market, and to the slow pay-down of mortgages and other debts.

As the world economy settles into this discouraging pattern, it is no surprise that hopes associated with the orthodox policies are fading. There is some recognition that those who said from the beginning that there would be "no return to normal" understood the situation, realizing that there had been structural failures in the strategic sectors. However, mainstream economics does not understand this. There are increasing calls for a "growth strategy" that would depart from the present austerity policies. This takes the form of demands for more monetary or fiscal expansion.[3] But these demands are not, generally, squared with the reality of higher resource costs and the uncertainties introduced by speculative markets and unstable prices. This is why, by themselves, these proposals lack credibility; they are not integrated, as they must be, into a new *strategic* approach.

Fixed Costs, Resource Costs, and the Half-Hidden Barriers to Recovery

In the present environment, it is useful to consider that the world's wealthy countries face *barriers to recovery*. These barriers represent specific problems that must be overcome, through institutional, political, legal, and in some instances scientific and engineering measures, as a condition of restoring economic prospects in a sustainable way. Speaking generally—but on the basis of a precise analytical theory—these barriers have to do with the high fixed costs of the present economic system, with rising resource costs in relation to those fixed costs, and with discount rates and uncertainty affecting the future outlook.[4]

Fixed costs are the consequence of past investments that must be maintained, social institutions *and* elements of the private economy that are able, through their control of state resources, to maintain themselves at the expense of final consumers, even though they deliver few (or no) goods that are actually consumed by either households or business. Fixed costs are necessary to extract resources efficiently from the environment, but they also impose a burden that narrows the scope for profitability of any private business endeavor. When fixed costs are excessive in relation to the cost of resources, profits are squeezed and may be negative—in which case private investment is likely to stop.

Some burdens of fixed cost are well-known, especially those imposed by the state,[5] such as an inefficient military or bureaucracy. This was the traditional problem of the European monarchies. Others arise when a vital infrastructure, such as a transport system, or a system providing health care or education, falls into disrepair or becomes too expensive to operate—a situation that (in addition to the military burden) contributed to the economic collapse of the Soviet Union. And others may arise when an ostensibly private sector providing intermediate goods or services exacts too large a toll on the operation of final producers. *This is the case of the financial sector in today's advanced economies.*

Thus, a first barrier to economic recovery in the wealthy countries is that the burden of the financial sector is too large. This barrier to recovery has four aspects.

In the first place, financial institutions impose large fixed costs on other enterprises; the revenues they extract are a direct charge to nonfinancial profits. Given a gross volume of profits available under the prevailing macroeconomic conditions, the division between financial and nonfinancial recipients is effectively a zero-sum game.[6] In the wake of the crisis, these institutions are generally unwilling to extend new commercial and industrial loans on favorable terms, as they consider the risks associated with nonfinancial expansion too high. That is partly because financial "services" cost too much.

Second, households in the United States and governments in the European periphery are burdened by unpayable debts. In the case of the United States this is compounded by very weak collateral, in the form of devalued housing. Meanwhile in Europe the credit markets have closed—arguably permanently—to smaller sovereigns. This is a situation unprecedented since the 1930s, in both regions, and for which no long-term cure is yet being advanced.

Third, the markets for securities created by the banks are tainted by the reputation for shady dealing that the banks now have, along with the lost credibility of the ratings agencies. This reduces liquidity in those markets and may well mean that they cannot recover their prior function. If that is the case, then alternative means for financing economic activity will need to be found.

Finally, the wealthy countries now lack alternative, low-cost ways to supply finance to business. Such institutions existed prominently in France, for example, in the postwar years but were dismantled or curtailed in the 1980s. In the United States the secondary mortgage market-makers Fannie Mae and Freddie Mac continue to exist, but with limited mandates that have prevented them from acting to resolve the foreclosure crisis. They also operate in that part of the credit economy—residential housing—that is least favorable to an early resumption of credit growth. Steps that were taken to cope with the collapse of credit in the 1930s, from the Reconstruction Finance Corporation to the Home Owners Loan Corporation and many others, remain to be emulated in today's political climate.

In the context of continuing high fixed financial costs, the second barrier is that rising *resource prices become a choke-chain on growth*. This is especially true when underregulated financial markets permit strong speculative influence over energy prices, translating anxieties about future supply and demand to the present. Increasing demand, even from a very low base, provokes energy-price instability, as a combination of producer strategies and apparent manipulation by commodity investors.

Increases in prices at the retail level (and therefore in imports) directly deplete business profits and so discourage investment. Further, *instability* in energy (and other resource) prices fosters *uncertainty* about the future path of recovery, effectively reducing *expected profits* adjusted for risk. The fear that prices will go higher weighs against investment in energy-consuming sectors; the fear that they may collapse weighs against sustained investment in renewables and other alternatives to fossil fuels. Both effects weigh on the future operations of the private sector, quite apart from increases in the real cost of energy production, a slower moving development. And all this is also quite apart from any constraints on energy use, due to climate change, that may be expected or imposed.

It follows that a sustained and collective effort to tame the energy marketplace—at a level of prices consistent with public purpose over the long term—is a prerequisite to stable recovery of private business activity. For this, high but stable prices would be better than high and unstable prices, because they would reduce, over time, the uncertainties associated with the business climate.

A third barrier to recovery is the self-inflicted wound of major fiscal cutbacks, which destroy public institutions—health care, education, transport—that are in fact technically viable and might otherwise remain so. The effect of cutbacks is to reduce the attractiveness of new investment, including foreign investment, while providing no effective relief to the domestic private sector. Meanwhile higher taxes drain away purchasing power, and emigration will begin to inflict serious losses of mobile and professional talent on some of the most affected nations.

In sum, the clear implication of this argument is that fixed costs must be reduced; the economic system must be made more efficient. The issue is how? And at whose expense?

The ongoing debate over budget priorities is *in effect* an argument over how to cut the burden of fixed costs—and on whom the burden of those cuts should fall. Those who benefit from direct, on-budget public provision of wages and education, and through public insurance schemes of health care and pensions oppose taking the full burden on themselves. *Nor should they do so*: if these costs are not paid by public agencies, they will continue to be incurred, in part, but on private accounts, and the total burden of the fixed cost could actually rise. Parents will pay for the education of children and children will pay for the care of parents, partly through private insurance—but less efficiently and with obvious severe results for those who cannot rely on such support.

In the case of transport and other services such as water and power, increasing returns and network economies generally assure that the least-cost way to provide the service is through a single public or para-public entity. Here, cutbacks can be a false economy; they reduce the use of the system, raise unit costs, and deepen the operating deficit. At some point, the case that the burden is not worth the expense becomes compelling. The effect of privatization in such circumstances is to replace a failed utility with an extractive monopoly, providing niche service at higher cost. Examples are legion.

Meanwhile the classification of finance as a private-sector activity obscures the close relationship between finance and state power. The financial draw on public resources is not continuous; the financial sector appears profitable until it crashes, and only then is it rescued at public expense. The test of such a rescue is whether it is done under terms that effectively increase private investment and control financial-sector costs—restoring nonfinancial profits and once again creating jobs. If the objective of policy is solely to maintain existing banks-in-being, this test is failed.

All of this suggests that neither market fundamentalism nor tax-cut Keynesianism will now work. Something broader, deeper, and more carefully thought out is required. *Fixed costs must be reduced, but on terms that are socially acceptable and fair, and that stabilize expectations about the long-term investment climate, given a realistic picture of the future of resource costs and the environmental constraint.* That is the challenge facing the leadership of the world's wealthy nations.

The Need for a Strategic Direction: Finance and Energy

What is needed is a *new strategic direction*, that is, *a clear line of policy for the long term and institutions to support it.* It must have two key components: a restructured financial sector and concerted, effective attention to the resource problem and to climate change. Both components would create jobs and foster more inclusive growth.

The financial sector should be shrunk, made more internally competitive, brought to justice as necessary, and its links to political power—through election finance, lobbying, and the revolving door—should be cut. There is precedent for this; it is not a new problem. Reforms comparable to those enacted in 1930s America and in much of postwar Europe are now once again required. The point here is one of the most elementary political economy: the scale and concentration of banks is inevitably the concentration of power and the subversion of a broadly based democratic state. "Wealth is power, as Mr. Hobbes says." So wrote Adam Smith in *Wealth of Nations*.

Other challenges include dealing with the complex and opaque world of financial derivatives, which are extremely difficult to regulate effectively in the information age. It is evident that these instruments are not necessary: the world got along well without them until recent decades. The evidence is plain that they do not do what their proponents allege, and that they cost more, to society at large, than they are worth. As Minsky pointed out, the major purpose of financial innovation is to evade regulations. The challenge for government is always to find an effective way of reimposing necessary regulation.

This is a problem that, at present, remains to be solved. It may be that the correct approach is simply to withdraw the support of the state for the enforcement of derivative bets; once the courts refuse to enforce them the market may fade away.

Energy—and the environment—is the fundamental physical challenge of the age. Since energy production alternatives are limited, and since expanded production of carbon-emitting energy sources is anyway untenable in the long run, the energy problem is primarily one of conservation and waste-reduction, for which there remains a large scope. But it is also one of regulating and supervising the futures markets, and of providing some control over prices through buffer stocks, and hence of stabilizing the economic climate going forward. To be politically acceptable, conservation must be facilitated by investments that make energy saving less onerous, providing ways to conserve energy while preserving living standards as far as possible.

This is the challenge. Within any given economy, it is a complex engineering problem requiring an independent, dedicated planning process, and investments at scale in suitable infrastructure. Between nations and between the developed and the developing worlds, it is a delicate challenge to diplomacy, negotiation, mutual understanding, and good faith. It would be foolish to promise success, but a key element in establishing a basis for hope is to clear the decks of international organizations such as the OECD for clear-minded consideration of the challenge.

And what of about public deficits and debt? Here is a major obstacle to clearing the mental decks. For a political person, the problem of public debt and deficits is unquestionably real. Anyone who comes up in politics through local and state government in the United States, or within the framework of the Maastricht Treaty in Europe, "knows" that budgets must be balanced and public debts kept within strict limits. They know this because it is a fact of constitutional, legal, and political life. It is also reinforced, through repetition, by many professional economists. But even this does not mean that, as a point of economics, it is true.

The conditions under which public debt is, or is not, sustainable are a topic for another paper.[7] Much (though not all) of the answer is institutional: debts are sustainable when they are owed by a sovereign in its own currency. Dangers arise only when they are owed by a sovereign in another currency or in a currency that the debtor cannot control. The first case explains why long-term interest rates have fallen to trivial levels in Japan, the United States, and other large countries; the second explains why countries in Latin America have come to avoid external debt, and the third is the essence of the Euro crisis.

Thus, one of the useful prerequisites for a new strategic vision would be to clarify, for the world, the distinction between *material sustainability*, which is a pressing challenge, and *public-finance sustainability*, which is (substantially) a smokescreen and a distraction.

Making Life Better

A pressing question remains: how to make life better in difficult times? The crisis happened. It cannot be wished away. In the aftermath, reforms, adjustments, and the reduction of fixed costs—public and private—are indispensable. Given the effects of the crisis, the industrialized countries should take an active approach to adjusting to the world as it is. Yet this is not hopeless: there is a *human component* that can improve the life prospects of those most affected, including elderly workers who are unemployed or anxious to retire, and younger workers who cannot find jobs because all available positions have been filled.

To that end, strengthening the public social insurance measures systems that industrialized countries already have, stronger family protection systems, better access to good education, and raising the relative wages of the least-well-paid workers would all be useful. Because the institutions that provide these services are relatively efficient, these are measures that do not increase—and may actually reduce—the material fixed costs of life. Further, because they are key elements of a fair and acceptable social compact, they can provide the necessary offset to the sacrifices that moving resources toward investment and conservation necessarily entail for current consumption. *In other words, the industrialized countries can and should offer their populations stability and security as compensation for accepting changes in the material structures of life.* This is the opposite of the policy direction of the past 30 years, which has emphasized gains in consumption as the reward for accepting instability and insecurity.[8]

A similar argument generalizes to favor broad movement toward more equal economic outcomes. Greater pay equality (up to a point) has been shown to be favorable per se to higher employment[9]; thus, measures that reduce inequality in pay structures can contribute to economic efficiency (in the fuller use of human resources) and also to competitiveness. The Scandinavian countries have understood this and made it a basis of their development for decades. Inside Europe, the challenge is to extend egalitarian structures of proven social effectiveness from the national to the international scale, offsetting and gradually shrinking the vast inequalities that exist across national borders in Europe.

In the United States, interregional inequalities have been sharply reduced, over 70 years, by the institutions of the New Deal and the Great Society. Today measures such as a right-to-rent law, a higher minimum wage,[10] and a window for earlier retirement and access to public health insurance for the present generation of older workers—so as to open vacancies for younger workers—would be effective, low-cost ways to relieve stress and adjust to the realities of the postcrisis world. In Europe analogous measures might include common unemployment insurance, a European Pension Union, providing a common minimum retirement standard across Europe, and a trans-European topping-up scheme, similar in its operation to the Earned Income Tax Credit in the United States.

In an uncertain, high-resource-cost world, adjustments are inevitable. But those advocating that the costs fall mainly on the low- and moderate-income population, through cuts in retirement, medical care, education, and public infrastructure, must realize that those affected will make the next move. Social upheaval is a possibility. *But reductions in fertility are a certainty.* They are, by far, the easiest way to defend living standards in the face of higher living costs. A transition from high fertility in the low-cost 1950s and 1960s to low fertility in the high-cost, energy-consuming countries after the 1970s has already occurred. It will deepen inexorably, if and as social protection is cut back.

These ideas are unconventional. But that, of course, is the point. They are in keeping with a consistent line of thought—a *paradigm*—that integrates resource flows, environmental constraints, and institutional trustworthiness into economic policy, and that examines the implications for the ordinary individuals who will have the final word. This is precisely what economics has lacked, and what it needs, if we are to restore prosperity on a more sustainable and inclusive basis.

Notes

The author thanks Jing Cheng for comments and Natica Smith for research assistance.

1. The United States took a notionally different path, enacting in 1978 the "Humphrey-Hawkins Full Employment and Balanced Growth Act," which stipulated "full employment, balanced growth...and reasonable price stability" as the objectives of economic policy, including for the Federal Reserve. (This writer drafted the Federal Reserve Act provisions of that bill.) However, the practical effect of this legislation was very slight.

2. Including the infamous 2003 press conference at which James Gilleran, director of the Office of Thrift Supervision, appeared with a stack of federal regulations and a chainsaw. His supervisory colleagues brought pruning shears.

3. Paul Krugman calls for monetary expansion; Lawrence Summers recently joined those calling for fiscal expansion.

4. This is not a chapter on formal economics, but readers interested in an effort to present the underlying analytical framework in a concise and systematic way may consult the references to Chen and Galbraith in the references section.

5. In *The Wealth of Nations*, Adam Smith conveyed the idea: "*Great nations are never impoverished by private, though they sometimes are by public prodigality and misconduct. The whole, or almost the whole public revenue, is in most countries employed in maintaining unproductive hands. Such are the people who compose a numerous and splendid court, a great ecclesiastical establishment, great fleets and armies, who in time of peace produce nothing, and in time of war acquire nothing which can compensate the expense of maintaining them, even while the war lasts*" (Book II, Chapter 3, para 30).

6. Formally, the Kalecki-Levy equation shows the macroeconomic determination of gross profits; the role and burden of the financial sector depends on the degree to which new investment facilitated by lending exceeds the revenues required to maintain the sector in being.

7. See my Levy Institute paper on this topic at: http://www.levyinstitute .org/pubs/pn_11_02.pdf.

8. It is likely that the policy proposed will be less attractive politically ex ante, because it is hard to give up the prospect of material gains, but more attractive ex post, because it will protect a larger number of people from penury. And it is only in retrospect that most people appreciate the low odds of winning a lottery.

9. See Galbraith and Garcilazo (2004) for details.

10. The idea of a substantially higher minimum wage has not been on the American agenda postcrisis, but it is beginning to attract the attention of a broad spectrum of observers, including the publisher of *The American Conservative*, the editorialist for *Bloomberg*, and a writer for the *Weekly Standard*.

CHAPTER 3

Labor Markets and Economic Development

Heiner Flassbeck

Thus writers in the classical tradition, overlooking the special assumption underlying their theory, have been driven inevitably to the conclusion, perfectly logical on their assumption, that apparent unemployment (...) must be due at bottom to a refusal by the unemployed factors to accept a reward which corresponds to their marginal productivity. A classical economist may sympathise with labour in refusing to accept a cut in its money-wage, and he will admit that it may not be wise to make it to meet conditions which are temporary; but scientific integrity forces him to declare that this refusal is, nevertheless, at the bottom of the trouble. (Keynes, 1936: 16)

Introduction

Flexibility of labor markets is the most important feature of the mantra of "structural policies" that have again been advocated in troubled countries after the big financial crisis. They were also the key message of the neoliberal revolution that did away with the welfare state and Keynesianism at the same time as rising unemployment during the 1970s. Sometimes it has been argued explicitly that globalization and technological progress require greater wage flexibility in the industrialized countries, given the pressures resulting from the competition of lower-paid workers in developing economies and/or from labor-saving technologies.

However, a deeper analysis reveals that neither increased international competition nor structural change inevitably lead to a distribution of income that favors the rich and deprives the poor. There are no natural or inevitable forces that would compel modern societies to tolerate rising inequality brought about by increased flexibility of the labor market. Indeed, the belief that only a more unequal outcome of the market process is an efficient one in a world of high unemployment and rapid change is the result of a misleading interpretation of the process of development in market economies. Actually, it is mainstream economic theory, not economic reality, that dominates the widespread perception that increased flexibility and rising inequality are "normal" outcomes of either the increased use of capital in the production process or "globalization." A better comprehension of the way in which a market economy evolves over time can open the way toward more equitable economic development, which would also generate more efficient market dynamics.

The stupendous importance of mainstream economic theory, deeply carved in most people's thinking about economic development, is demonstrated by the fact that, on the one hand, the trend toward greater inequality is being increasingly criticized, while, on the other, the "structural" measures that are proposed by the mainstream and applied in many countries to overcome the crises are again based on wage cutting and an attempt to foster investment by means of rising inequality. In fact, this pattern has shaped most of the past 35 years and explains, to very large extent, the trend toward greater inequality in a world of high unemployment and increasingly frequent shocks and crises. But the conventional medicine of introducing greater flexibility in wage setting has worsened the illness of inequality without healing the one of unemployment. This is why revamping the old theories will not help the patient; only a new theoretical approach and a totally different therapy can bring relief.

A Simple Story of Supply and Demand

Imagine a market where no market-clearing price is found and a huge supply surplus remains at the end of a day of trading. Without further information, a well-trained economist would conclude that due to a certain shock prices must have gone up the day before and that at these elevated prices there was not enough demand to fully absorb the supply. Provided with the additional information that on the previous days prices actually had gone down, the economist would conclude that something extraordinary must have happened: For some reason supply has increased or demand for the good has collapsed on that very day and prices were not flexible enough to balance that out. Which forces may have caused supply to go up or demand to go down from one day to another? Finding evidence that supply hardly changed on this market, the economist would then conclude that only a sudden drop in demand could have caused the supply surplus to emerge. He would also conclude that the drop in demand must have exogenous reasons, that is, reasons that lie outside the specific market itself, as prices had not risen during the days before the demand shock occurred. Our economist would be confident, nevertheless, that a further drop in prices would reequilibrate this market, even though he would concede that producers on that market are suffering from an event that they are not liable for.

Putting a bit more life into this story, we may assume not one but two markets, one for bread and the other for meat, where meat shall be the market were the shock occurs. Assume that the fall in demand for meat was induced by a rumor among the bakers in the city that the consumption of meat is dangerous these days due to a virus that has infected many animals. On the day this rumor spreads the bakers sharply reduce their consumption of meat. Market forces work and lead to a sharp fall of the price of meat from its already low level. This will not immediately restore demand but it will reduce the income of the meat suppliers, the butchers. Consequently, these have to restrain their demand for goods from other markets. If bread is their most important consumption item, they will reduce their demand for bread the following day. The price for bread will then fall to a level where the demand of butchers is restored in quantitative terms. However, the bakers will now have a lower income than before so that they are forced to buy much less meat than before the shock, even if it turns out that have reacted to a false rumor. No doubt, both bakers and butchers will find a new equilibrium, but this will be at a much lower level of production and provide all of them with a much lower income than before. Without a new shock in the opposite direction or intervention from outside, the market will be stuck at this lower price level even if after a while everybody understands what happened.

A well-trained economist quickly understands what is wrong with this story. He would point to the fact that in the real world the butchers, by lowering their prices, would normally quickly find other customers, whose income has remained unchanged and who are induced by the lower price to buy and consume more meat. With a price elasticity of demand in the range of one the increase in quantity would fully offset the fall in prices. When the bakers are coming back to the market as customers, the old equilibrium will eventually be restored. The economist would argue that the traditional demand/supply mechanism is valid only if demand and supply curves for each product are independent. Moreover, he would insist that this case represents the real world with many market participants much better than the example given earlier, where the bakers' supply is not independent of their demand. In his view, the bakers demanding less meat temporarily, thereby reducing the income of the butchers and, thus, the latter's demand for bread is a special case that does not represent the conditions in the overall economy.

This is true. Only if there is one product whose supply and demand curves are not independent of each other (because a fall of the price of this product would reduce the demand for all other products simultaneously) would it be justified to assume that under certain circumstances the overall economy tends to be destabilized by flexible prices because the supply-and-demand mechanism would not work in the traditional way.

And indeed, this product does exist. There is one product that is demanded as an indispensable input for the production of all goods and services; the income of those offering this product—or factor of production—affects the demand for any other good or service that is produced in a modern economy. This factor of production is labor. It is needed for the production of every part of the supply of the overall economy, and the demand from those earning a labor income is needed to sell this supply and make the production process economically viable. The price that is paid for labor as an input factor (in the form of wages) is not independent of the ability of labor to buy the output resulting from the combination of labor and capital in the production process. By the same token, the quantity of output that can be sold depends on the price paid for labor.

Now imagine a world with an initial equilibrium, at which all those who want to work are employed. But due to a shock originating outside the labor market the demand for labor suddenly falls, that is, unemployment rises. The surplus supply of labor would put downward pressure on the price of labor and allow employers to reduce wages. With falling wages but high unemployment the demand for most products would fall immediately, and this would further depress the willingness of companies to hire workers, notwithstanding the lower wages. According to the orthodox view, workers would try to get back to work by accepting wage cuts. But this cannot work because lower wages will further reduce overall demand, as shown in the baker/butcher example earlier. In this situation, a major destabilization of the economy can be avoided only if overall demand is increased by the government (or if the savings ratio is reduced as a result of another exogenous shock).

One may argue that the emergence of a global shock that leads to a significant rise in unemployment is highly improbable. However, this is exactly what happened to the developed economies in the aftermath of the "Great Recession" following the financial crisis of 2008. For all developed economies taken together, unemployment after the financial crisis shot up to

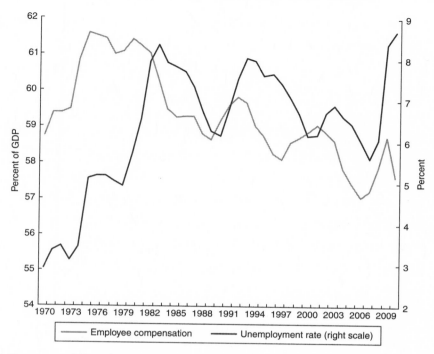

Figure 3.1 Wage share and unemployment in the developed economies.

9 percent in 2008/2009, the highest level of the past 60 years, and this happened although the share of wages in GDP was lower than at any time since World War II.

Since the beginning of the Great Recession in 2009 unemployment has again become the most pressing economic problem for the global economy. According to neoclassical theory this should not have happened. The fact that just ahead of the new big jump in unemployment the share of wages in overall GDP was extremely low impressively refutes the idea that wages are just a price that equilibrates supply and demand in the labor market. The observation that unemployment has risen to higher levels than in any other recession during the past three decades, even though wages have been lower than ever before in this period, proves that something must be wrong with the neoclassical theory of the labor market.

Real Wages Do Not Determine Employment

When wage shares rose sharply in the 1970s in tandem with falling employment and skyrocketing unemployment, this motivated the return of economic thinking to what had been a mainstream model in the 1920s already. In this approach, the main reason for unemployment is seen in the unwillingness of workers to accept lower wages when circumstances change. Consequently, too little inequality and the resistance of trade unions to accept the "need" of lowering wages was more and more considered to be the main culprit for the new and persistent unemployment problem.

Among the international institutions it was mainly the OECD that championed the revival of this old approach. Its recommendations go a long way in explaining the rise in inequality in the developed world during the last three decades. In its *Jobs Study* of 1994 the organization describes the mechanism that should lead to superior results in the labor market as follows:

> The adjustment process itself depends on the interplay of employers' demand for labour, which will be negatively related to the level of real wages, and the desire to be employed, which will be positively related to the level of real wages. In principle, there will be a real wage level—or, more correctly, a level of real labour costs—that ensures that all who want to work at that wage will find employment. (OECD, 1994, Part I: 69)

And elsewhere: "Self-equilibration in the labour market requires, in addition to a negative relationship between labour-demand and labour costs, that wages respond to market conditions: labour-market slack putting downward pressure on real wages and vice versa" (OECD, 1994, Part II: 3).

As mentioned earlier, whatever the reasons for the rise in unemployment, a large number of unemployed workers exerts enormous pressure on wages as the balance of negotiating power shifts in favor of employers. Workers threatened by unemployment are normally willing to sacrifice their share of the productivity increase or even to accept a reduction of their income in an attempt to secure their jobs. However, what in the conventional view appears to confirm the proper working of the market mechanism, in reality is a destabilizing factor for the overall economy. While in a normal goods market a supply surplus is expected to induce a fall of the price of the respective good and an increase in the quantity demanded, the fall of the price in the labor market creates a new problem.

In the United States, for example, wages lagged behind productivity for many years preceding the crisis, and the median wage did not increase for decades. When the crisis hit in 2008 and 2009 unemployment rose at least as sharply as in former recessions, and it seems to be more persistent than ever before after the bottoming out of the recession. But if unemployment can rise sharply although real wages have been lagging behind productivity, the simple market nexus of real wages and employment does not apply. Indeed, this implies that the assumption that lower wages will increase employment and reduce unemployment is not warranted. Today, there is widespread doubt whether wage cuts in countries where the recovery is fragile, as in the United States, can improve the situation or will actually worsen it further. Would it not be plausible that companies adjust their production further downward if the first-round effect of a fall in nominal wages is a drop in the demand of most households, since such a drop would reduce their capacity utilization?

The crucial point is the sequence of events. Economists tend to tell the result of downward wage adjustments in a recession from the point of view of given supply-and-demand schedules with normal price elasticities. But the a priori belief in the logic of normal supply-and-demand curves cannot guide a proper judgment of how employment in the economy as a whole will react to lower wages. In an economy evolving over time under the conditions of objective uncertainty (the state of "nonergodic development," as explained by Paul Davidson in this volume) no single player has meta-information concerning the outcome of complex processes that would allow him to react in a different way than others in the case of exogenous shocks.

Take the case of a general fall of (nominal) wages triggered by a recession and rising unemployment. In this situation households will expect a fall of their income in real terms. With this expectation, they would immediately reduce their consumption in an attempt to avoid a deterioration of their balance sheets. For employers, at first glance, falling wages would seem to bring relief from the pressure on profits resulting from falling demand in the recession. However, if reduced household demand depresses their business even further and exerts additional pressure on prices, this relief is a mixed blessing. Faced with even stronger pressure on prices and falling demand, the average firm will refrain from taking strategic decisions that would imply an increased use of both labor and capital. Expecting the average firm to engage in a restructuring process using more labor and less capital, as suggested by the neoclassical employment theory, is naïve, to say the least.

A process in which falling nominal wages signal to every individual firm a lasting fall of real wages and a lasting change in the relative prices of labor and capital, which might induce firms to substitute capital for labor, is mere fiction. This process would have to be extremely rapid, and all firms would have to engage in it simultaneously. Only an instantaneous transition from one production structure to the other would prevent a reduction of overall demand. Falling demand, however, fundamentally alters the conditions under which firms adjust to the change in relative prices of the factors of production. If wages per hour fall and the growth in the number of hours worked does not compensate fully for the fall in wages, the wage sum in the economy will fall and, with very high probability, induce a drop in demand.

A similar argument has to be made concerning the less sophisticated theoretical idea stipulating that lower nominal wages will shift income from wages to profits, thereby motivating additional investment. However, such a simple shift can occur only under the condition that overall demand remains unchanged. But this condition is not fulfilled in reality. Again, the sequence of events is crucial: If demand falls immediately after the drop in wages,[1] the expected substitution of falling wages by higher profits is impossible, because overall output and, thus, profits will be reduced. Such a scenario will be prevented only when the savings ratio of workers, and households more generally, falls or when the government increases its budget deficit.

While this analysis holds for closed economies, it seems to be less clear-cut for open economies with an important share of exports in their overall demand. Under certain circumstances exports of such economies may indeed expand in reaction to wage cuts. If wages are reduced in a single country, if the productivity trend of that country is unchanged, and if the currency of that country does not appreciate to an extent that compensates for the fall in wages, then exports may be stimulated. The overall effect on demand, however, depends on the relative weight of exports compared to that of domestic demand. For very open economies the net effect may be positive. Moreover, as the competitiveness of domestic producers improves in such a scenario, this can have a lasting effect on export demand: the producers of that country gain market shares and thus benefit from global demand growth more than proportionally. On the other hand, continued real depreciation by means of wage cuts may massively distort international trade and create huge payments imbalances as the effects on competitiveness accumulate, creating a huge absolute advantage of the country over time.

However, the larger an economy and the more important its exports and imports are for the global economy, the less will that country be able to sustain a policy of appropriation of market shares through wage dumping. Its trading partners will start retaliating by cutting wages too, or by forcing a depreciation of their exchange rate, or by erecting protectionist barriers.

Box 3.1   The German miracle

Inside the European Monetary Union (EMU) Germany, the largest economy, has researched wage reductions to fight high and persistent unemployment. As work time reduction schemes and other measures had failed to reduce unemployment, policymakers, employers, and union leaders agreed in 1999 to abandon the traditional formula that anchored nominal wage growth in the trend of productivity growth plus the inflation target. The idea was to make productivity growth available "for employment growth." The new German labor market approach coincided with the start of EMU and brought about a huge divergence in unit labor cost growth among the members of the currency union.

German unit labor costs and prices rose consistently at a rate below the commonly agreed inflation target of 2 percent. On the other side, in most southern European countries nominal wage growth exceeded national productivity growth and the inflation target of EMU by a small but rather stable margin. France was the only country to exactly meet the agreed path for nominal wage growth. The small annual divergences in price and wage growth accumulated to create a huge gap in competitiveness over time. At the end of the first decade of EMU the cost and price gap between Germany and southern Europe amounted to some 25 percent, and between Germany and France to 15 percent. In other words, Germany's real exchange rate depreciated quite significantly, despite the absence of national currencies.

This had an enormous impact on trade flows. Germany's exports flourished and its imports slowed down. Southern Europe and France experienced widening trade and current account deficits. While at the beginning of the currency union, and in many years before that, trade among the members had been rather balanced, the first decade of EMU was a period of dramatically rising imbalances. Even after the shock of the financial crisis and its devastating effects on global trade (which affected Germany more than the other countries), the German trade surplus was quickly restored, to about €170 billion per year, with about €80 billion against the other EMU countries.

On the other side, the deep recession and the austerity programs in the deficit countries tend to reduce their visible deficits, but this does not reflect a rapid and fundamental turnaround in competitiveness. Moreover, the economies in crisis lack the stimulus to revive growth. The lesson is simple: absolute and accumulating advantages of one country against a group of similar countries are unsustainable. A huge gap in competitiveness has to be closed sooner or later. Failure to do so will create uncertainty on the side of lenders and tend to increase interest rates. In order to make net repayments on their debt, the indebted countries have to have a chance to generate current-account surpluses. But if the creditor countries defend their surplus positions by all means, default of debtors in unavoidable.

The model used in Germany was used as an analogy with the competition of companies. However, the conditions for competition of companies do not apply to countries, in particular not to countries with independent currencies. Companies able to generate higher productivity through innovation can produce at lower unit labor costs than their competitors, but this mechanism does not work among entire economies, because in a world with national currencies and national monetary policy, a country supplying its goods at much lower prices would gain market shares and accumulate huge trade and current account surpluses. Political pressure to adjust wages and prices in international currency would mount, and sooner or later the country would be forced to adjust its wages, measured in international currency, through a revaluation of its currency.

In a currency union the member countries explicitly or implicitly agree not to go the deflationary or inflationary way (i.e., to follow a path of nominal wage growth below or above national productivity growth plus the commonly agreed inflation target). With an inflation target of close to 2 percent (as established by the ECB for the Euro zone) the implicit contract was that nominal wages would not rise faster than national productivity plus these 2 percent. This implies that each country can use its productivity increase, be it 1 percent like in Germany or 2 like in Greece, for augmenting real wages or reducing working hours, or a combination of both. If one member deviates from this path upward or downward it creates an externally unsustainable situation.

To be sure, the German approach to create a favorable competitive position for its producers by very low wage growth in relation to the progress of productivity has not been successful. Inside Germany it has undermined the dynamics of the domestic markets, and at the European level it has increased the vulnerability of Germany's trading partners, something that can be expected to have negative repercussions on Germany itself. While the country's exports exploded sometime after the introduction of EMU, domestic demand remained as flat as real wages. This clearly proves that the neoclassical nexus stipulating a substitution of capital by labor and rising employment is wrong. If this nexus really worked, the wage sum of workers in real terms would have grown in line with productivity growth. The apparent success of the German experiment was due only to the historically unique situation of the currency union and the false tolerance of the partners in the first decade of EMU.

Overall, the result of the German experiment was disastrous for the southern European countries and France as they lost international market shares without having a chance to successfully retaliate the German attack. With German politics and wage-negotiating partners refusing to move toward higher wages, the deficit countries are forced to cut wages by a wide margin to get back into the markets. However, as falling wages mean a fall in domestic demand that cannot be fully compensated by higher exports in countries with fairly small export shares (in the order of 25 percent of GDP in the case of Italy and Spain), the resulting depression leads to political disaster, as Greece has amply shown.

The crucial nexus for lasting success in open and in closed economies is the one between money wages (nominal wages) and employment. The economy as a whole can create a demand that is sufficiently high to assure full employment of the human and technical capacities only when money wages are rising strictly in line with the productivity trend plus the inflation target. To be sure this approach keeps the wage share constant, but cannot by itself correct the effects of wage restraint in the past.

While this is straightforward, negative supply shocks, although rather rare at the level of the overall economy, have a logic of their own. The most frequently quoted examples from the past have been the oil shocks hitting the world economy in the 1970s and at the beginning of the 1980s. To the surprise of mainstream economists, countries with relatively rigid wages and wage structures like Germany were the most successful in preventing an acceleration of inflation as a result of the original shock of sharply rising oil import prices. The reason is easy to understand: rigidity of wages means rigidity of *nominal* wages, but flexibility of *real* wages. In countries with flexible nominal wages a one-off price shock on the goods market translates into higher inflation (which means a permanently higher *increase* of the price level). This is because the spark of inflation jumps from imports and the goods market to the labor market. This happens when nominal wages are indexed to the *actual* rate of inflation, as in many countries with backward-looking indexation schemes, such as the *scala mobile* in Italy. Such schemes are designed to prevent a fall of real wages and to protect workers from redistribution of income through inflation. However, this protection is given even in the event of an untypical inflationary acceleration that results from redistribution in favor of a third party, in this case the foreign suppliers of oil. The domestic producers who bore the brunt of the cost of higher import prices in the first round passed the second-round effect of higher wag again on to prices and, in this way, turned a one-off price shock into a permanently higher inflation rate. This, in turn, prompted restrictive action by the central bank. Restrictive monetary policies then created a demand shock that led to the fall of employment.

Rigidity of nominal wages is preferable in a situation when the economy has to adjust to a negative supply shock. It provides the flexibility of real wages that is required to avoid permanently higher inflation triggered by an inflationary bout. This helps to prevent an additional demand shock resulting from restrictive monetary policies to fight inflation. Thus, the macroeconomics of wages and the labor market are clear and straightforward: Rigidity of nominal wages, in the sense of nominal wage adjustments in line with the inflation *target* and the productivity *trend*, is the preferred rule of adjustment to both demand shocks and supply shocks.

Growth, Not the Real Wage, Determines Employment

This analysis has important consequences for economic policy. As the simple supply-demand mechanism is not operating in the economy-wide labor market, a rise in unemployment cannot be prevented by means of flexible wages. In fact, the creation of new employment is a positive function of output growth, not of falling wages and a deteriorating wage share. Analyzing the labor market in isolation, instead of relating it to the overall income stream, involves a grave error. For most countries in the world, but for developed countries in particular, as has been shown repeatedly by UNCTAD, employment cycles are very closely associated with cycles of output growth.

There can be no doubt that sustained recoveries are needed to reduce unemployment. On the other hand, a downswing like the Great Recession of 2008 and 2009 destroys employment even when wage flexibility is very high and the wage share is very low. The fact that macroeconomic environments have diverged among similar countries over time is owed to different macroeconomic approaches rather than to different degrees of wage flexibility. Indeed, in the years of relatively high employment growth during the 1970s and the 1980s there was much less wage restraint than during the last two decades. The latter, however, show a meager result in terms of employment compared with the former.

Even more perplexing in light of the neoclassical proposition of a wage-employment nexus based on the substitution of capital by labor is the strong positive correlation between investment in fixed capital and employment creation. It is evident that companies in the real world invest and disinvest in labor and capital at the same time and not in labor *or* capital. This evidence directly refutes both the substitution thesis and the role of relative prices. Capital and labor are complementary factors that are combined to achieve a certain output independent of their relative prices.

Clearly, the elasticity of employment in relation to growth differs from country to country, and from period to period, but the close link between growth, employment, and investment defies the belief that a significant number of new jobs can be created without a critical level of investment and output growth. Once it is recognized that it is not the relative cost of labor but the pace of output growth that is the key determinant of the level of employment, it follows that investment in real productive capacity, and the demand expansion that motivates such investment, are the main drivers of both income growth and employment creation.

Whether or not aggregate demand expands sufficiently to assure employment of all people willing to work depends on the distribution of the gains from productivity growth. The policies generally adopted over the past 25 years have sought to keep wages low and have served to translate productivity gains either into higher capital income or into lower output prices. But, as shown earlier, wage compression as a means to generate higher profits is self-defeating: unless the purchasing power of wage earners increases, demand growth will be insufficient to achieve full employment of all existing productive capacities.

If the purchasing power of domestic wage earners does not increase sufficiently, the only way out is to stimulate exports through falling wages and improved competitiveness. But this creates a fallacy of composition. Competitiveness is a relative concept: not all countries can improve their competitiveness at the same time. Employment creation at the expense of growth and employment generation in other countries creates unsustainable debt accumulation in the deficit countries. Therefore, what holds for any single country over the medium term also holds for the world economy as a whole: Real wage growth in line with productivity growth is indispensible for a sustained pace of expansion of global effective demand at which all productive resources are fully utilized and for nourishing a virtuous cycle of growth, investment, productivity increases, and employment over time.

If dysfunctional flexibility of nominal wages is avoided and nominal wages in all countries broadly follow what could be called the "golden growth rule" described earlier, the wage share remains constant and most groups of society fully participate in the progress of the economy. With this rule the overall growth of nominal unit labor costs equals the inflation rate. For the developed countries this is true for long periods in history, including in particular those periods when a sufficient number of jobs were created and unemployment was on the retreat.

The participation of the majority of the people in the gains from productivity growth is crucial because their growing income is the main source of consumption of domestically produced goods and services. The dynamics of investment in a broad range of activities can unfold only if the proceeds of all productive activities are channeled through the pockets of all income groups. There can be no doubt that successful strategies for inclusive income growth and employment generation depend on investment in fixed capital. In economies with a dominant private sector, such investment is strongly influenced by the growth of demand for the goods and services that are produced and by the conditions to finance such investment. On both sides, supportive public policies play a key role.

For this purpose, new policy instruments have to be devised. Supportive monetary, financial, and fiscal policies are required to achieve strong growth based on fixed capital formation. However, it has been overlooked that the task of these policies to support employment growth can be greatly facilitated by the additional use of an incomes policy that builds on certain rules for determining mass incomes in a growing economy. If well designed, an incomes policy can contribute to employment growth by enabling a steady expansion of domestic demand. The implementation of an incomes policy requires an institutional framework adapted to the economic structure and the historical specificities of each country. Such an institutional framework is all the more important as an incomes policy can serve not only as an instrument to support employment generation but also as a means to control inflation. Wage growth according to the golden rule directly contributes to low and stable inflation and prevents demand from increasing faster than the supply potential.

Many countries have a history of very high inflation due to bouts of inflation spilling over to nominal wage increases through backward-looking indexation mechanisms. This has proved to be extremely costly, because central banks aiming to bring inflation down against permanent upward price pressures from the cost side have to produce shocks for the real economy through interest rate hikes. This implies sacrificing real investment and employment for the sake of nominal stabilization. Anchoring of nominal wages in the productivity growth trend, adjusted for an inflation target, helps avoid this.

Economic Policy Is Key for Employment Growth

Flexibility of the labor market, the mantra of the neoliberal counterrevolution of the last decades, is predicated on a model of the economy that does not resemble the world we live in. In reality, there is no static equilibrium in the labor market that would be easily reinstalled after a shock by means of flexible wages. Efficient dynamic adjustment to shocks in an economy operating under objective uncertainty is a totally different matter. An approach that focuses on these dynamics recognizes not only that the preferences and the income of the majority of the population must be the main concern of economic reasoning, but also that these are the main drivers of the dynamics of the system. In such an approach the notion of flexibility loses all its fascination.

At the macro level the use of flexible wages and more inequality as a remedy for unemployment is definitively ineffective if the economy is facing the most frequent shock, namely, a demand shock. While dealing with huge macroeconomically relevant supply shocks like an oil price shock requires some kind of passive flexibility on the part of workers, the conventionally propagated microeconomic or sectoral flexibility of wages and the resulting redistribution are ineffective. What is needed in support of the dynamics of modern market systems are flexible profits, not flexible wages, because the latter reduce the incentives for innovative investment by firms. In the real world shocks are mainly absorbed by profits rather than wages. This observation applies to all sorts of shocks, including those that emanate from foreign trade and foreign direct investment. Changes in profits lead the economy into the right direction to face the next challenge instead of restoring the unrestorable. The static neoclassical model of separated labor markets with flexible wages that regularly produce inequality in case of adjustment to shocks, be they international or intertemporal, is not relevant and should not guide the policies of adjustment at any stage of development.

The International Framework for Effective Wage Adjustment

There can be no doubt: to be efficient, the adjustment process in developed and developing countries alike has to be entrenched into a rational global or regional monetary system. Otherwise, external macro shocks threaten the smooth adjustment described earlier. For macroeconomic shocks to be buffered, nominal exchange rates have to follow strictly the fundamentals of the countries involved, that is, the differential in inflation or unit labor costs. In this way, unit labor costs determined at the national level can be equalized in international currency. This is the most effective instrument to avoid huge macroeconomic shocks, such as an overvaluation of the real exchange rate, and their potential to generate downward pressure on wages and more inequality.

Unfortunately, an exchange rate system that leaves the valuation of currencies entirely to the market (free floating) does not work properly as currency speculation and short-term investment tend to drive exchange rates away from their fair values (Flassbeck, 2001; UNCTAD, 2011). The search for arbitrage from interest rate differentials across currencies, the so-called carry trade, dominates the markets and frequently causes currencies of countries with high inflation and, consequently, high interest rates to appreciate. Therefore, considerably strengthened global monetary cooperation is indispensable in order to create a level playing field in international trade.

Macroeconomic Policies and Labor Market Flexibility

A number of institutional arrangements are necessary to achieve the rigidity of nominal wages as recommended here. Most important is government support for the creation and strengthening of trade unions with a nationwide mandate. The principle of equal pay for equal work in different firms and segments of the labor market can only be enforced by strong unions with a very broad mandate, especially in economies with a fairly low mobility of labor.

Additionally, protection of workers against the permanent pressure to "price themselves back into the market" (OECD) is crucial for successful adjustment. The social aspects of protecting workers against prolonged phases of unemployment are important, but even more so are the economic aspects. In order to prevent the repercussions on wages caused by high unemployment following shocks on the goods or financial markets, a tight safety net is needed that would allow temporarily unemployed workers to search for jobs elsewhere in the economy provided that major cuts in their standard of living can be prevented.

Bold government action to tackle rising unemployment not only minimizes uncertainty and threat for workers, but also the risk that the economy slips into a second dip as a result of pressure on wages and falling domestic demand. Indeed, the more aggressive stance of economic policy in the United States has long been seen as a substitute to the more advanced social safety nets in many European countries and their more sophisticated unemployment insurance schemes.

In general, as the market mechanism cannot remedy rising unemployment, the role of governments in stabilizing the overall economy becomes crucial for employment creation and income distribution. Governments can prevent the huge additional costs that arise if the pressure on wages stemming from high unemployment is allowed to permeate the whole economy. The negative second-round effects of a fall in wages or the wage share on domestic demand can and should be avoided by all means.

This result must sound perplexing to those who have grown up with the conventional idea that the labor market is governed by normal supply-and-demand curves. But even for those who believe in the logic of the market the fact that recently unemployment has risen throughout the developed world without any increase of the wage share—actually, it was accompanied by a fall of the wage share—should be reason enough to reflect their position. If the labor market can easily get out of "equilibrium" without involvement of the prices on that market, there is no argument to conclude that the way back to equilibrium would be possible through a further fall of these prices. Currently, the most striking cases in point are to be found in the Euro zone. In the southern European members of the zone unemployment has exploded despite enormous wage cuts. Thus, the popular proposition that in order to solve their problems these countries need more labor flexibility is a mere reflection of the old static view that has to be conquered to find cogent solutions for a world of change and development.

Box 3.2 Why minimum wages are indispensible

Government-determined minimum wages are a fact of life in most developed and developing economies. In particular, countries that lack a tightly knit social safety net have frequently chosen the instrument of legal minimum wages to protect low-skilled workers from being exploited by powerful patrons, in particular in times of long lasting and high unemployment. In the view of mainstream economists, wage setting by the government is an intervention in an efficient market and, since their reasoning is grounded in a model with normally shaped supply-and-demand curves, they assert that this intervention comes with the risk of creating even more unemployment, despite considerable empirical evidence to the contrary. It is argued that since the government may set a wage that is higher than the supposed equilibrium price of labor, which, in the neoclassical world, is determined by the marginal productivity of the workers, it actually exposes the low-skilled workers it intends to protect to a much higher risk of unemployment.

However, marginal productivity is a theoretical concept based on the idea that the contribution of, for example, one hour of work of a certain worker is measurable and clearly identifiable. If the law of one price is valid for a given segment of the labor market, all workers in that segment have to accept a wage cut if one additional hour is added to the work process and the output produced in that additional hour is lower than the output produced during the previous hours (which is called a production process with diminishing returns to scale). The concept of marginal productivity wages would be valid only if the inputs of many different employees into the production process were extremely standardized and could be clearly identified and measured. This, however, is not at all the case in most modern production settings.

The huge majority of employees are working in an environment where neither the marginal contributions of individual members of a production team nor their relative contributions are known and could be measured. For example, what is the marginal productivity of a nurse in a hospital and what is her relative contribution to the overall outcome compared to that of the chief surgeon or the chief of administration? Because this is unknown, most of the employees in modern societies receive a remuneration that reflects roughly the scarcity and availability of people with a similar qualification, rather than individual marginal productivities. Productivity increases in particular production processes adding up to the increase in the overall productivity of the economy is typically reflected in falling prices of the goods that are produced more efficiently. The lower-than-expected inflation would increase the real wage of *all* employees even though there has been no improvement in the individual productivity of each employee. It is the team—and, in this extreme version, the team of the whole economy—that is rewarded by the progress of the team as a whole, while the improvements of the productivity of individual workers in that process may not even be noticed.

Take the example of a teacher at an elementary school, who teaches for 40 years always exactly the same things without any innovation or an increase in his or her individual productivity and without any change in the nominal salary. With rising overall productivity in the economy as a whole the teacher will nevertheless enjoy rising purchasing power if the economy-wide progress in productivity is allowed to permeate the economy in the form of a falling price level.

Therefore, all societies have a wide range within which they can determine a minimum wage without violating any market law or the principle of supply and demand. If, for example, there would be a rule that the minimum wage should always be half of the average wage of the economy under consideration, it is hard to see how such an arrangement would increase the risk of some groups becoming unemployed. Some labor intensive goods and services would become more expensive but the purchasing power of a large group of employees would rise, and with it the levels of aggregate demand, economy-wide production, and employment.

As shown by a number of countries, minimum wages and their regular adjustment can provide important indications for wage negotiations in the private sector. A minimum wage indexed to the productivity trend and the target for inflation can act as a stabilizer of income expectations of the majority of dependent workers, thereby helping to stabilize the growth trajectory of domestic demand and at the same time to keep inflation close to the target rate. Participation of workers, rather than labor market flexibility, is the formula for success in developed and developing countries alike.

Conclusion

The experience of the neoliberal reform agendas of the 1980s and 1990s has shown that capital accumulation, productivity growth, and job creation do not automatically result from a market-dominated process combined with policies to foster what the mainstream considers to be "market forces." The efficient allocation of resources through flexible markets and flexible market prices, which form the body of mainstream economic theory, plays only a minor role in the dynamics of an efficient market economy. Much more important than static allocation are arrangements that allow innovative investors to shape the process of structural change and lead the economy toward higher levels of activity.

The labor market is concerned by these arrangements in a number of ways. The most important one is the provision that the growth rate of average real wages remains in line with the overall performance of the economy (i.e., the growth of labor productivity), because this stabilizes overall demand. Additionally, an arrangement that provides for regular adjustments of nominal wages, which also reflect the official inflation target, stabilizes the inflation rate and allows monetary policy be more closely geared toward the stimulation of investment. These rules should be complemented by an arrangement warranting similarity of the wage level for similar qualifications across the economy, thereby establishing the right incentives for investors in fixed capital.

All these considerations and arguments are in stark contrast to the new "flexibility hype." Despite the failure of labor market flexibilization to solve the unemployment problem in the past, this hype came in response to the new spike in unemployment in the aftermath of the financial crisis. But the obvious failure to bring the global economy back on a sustainable growth path after 2008, and in particular the failure to revive domestic demand in the developed world, should be taken as a wake-up call. If the majority of the population loses faith in the willingness of employers and governments to provide them with a fair share of the collectively produced income, the growth of that overall income itself will suffer drastically. Relearning some old lessons about fairness and participation will eventually be the only way to overcome the crisis and to return to sustained economic growth.

Notes

This chapter draws on Chapter V of the Trade and Development Report of UNCTAD of 2012, which was authored by Heiner Flassbeck.

1. Demand could even fall *before* wages actually come down. If such the possibility of a wage reduction is broadly discussed among union members or accompanied by strikes and demonstrations, households may cut their demand in advance to accommodate the expected wage cut.

CHAPTER 4

Balance Sheet Recessions and the Global Economic Crisis

Richard Koo

E conomists in the United States, Europe, and Japan differ sharply on what constitutes the correct policy response to the economic crisis. This divergence in views stems from the fact that these economies are suffering from a rare type of recession, which has largely been overlooked by the economics profession. Economists, who constructed elaborate theories based on the assumption that the private sector would always aim at maximizing profits, never anticipated the scenario of a private sector seeking to minimize debt. But when a debt-financed asset price bubble bursts, the private sector is left with a huge debt overhang, and to climb out of this state of negative equity it must pay down debt or increase savings, even if interest rates are zero. When the private sector as a whole is minimizing debt, the economy continuously loses aggregate demand equivalent to the saved but unborrowed amount. This situation has come to be known as a *balance sheet recession*.

Deleveraging-Driven Recession Leads to Prolonged Slump

A recurring concern in Western economies today is that they may be headed for a "lost decade" similar to the Japanese experience in the 1990s. The fact that it has not been possible over four years of near-zero interest rates and massive quantitative easing to bring the economies back to health has added to worries and confusion in the policy debate. With a bewildering array of often contradictory proposals coming from well-known economists, the situation resembles doctors arguing over how to treat a patient who is not responding to conventional measures. With so much disagreement among the experts, it is hardly surprising that political leaders on both sides of the Atlantic are confused.

Fortunately for the West, the same policy debate took place in Japan more than a decade ago and led to similar animosity and confusion. After many years of sometimes acrimonious debate, it was discovered that the nation's recession was not an ordinary recession and that a very different policy response was needed to overcome it.

The key difference between an ordinary recession and one that can produce a lost decade is that in the latter, a large portion of the private sector is *minimizing debt* instead of maximizing profits in an attempt to remove the debt overhang created by the bursting of a debt-financed asset price bubble. With balance sheets underwater, these businesses and households have no choice but to reduce debt regardless of the level of interest rates. When the private sector deleverages even though interest rates are at zero, the economy enters a deflationary spiral because, with no one to borrow and spend money, it *continuously* loses demand equal to the unborrowed savings.

To see this, consider a world where a household has an income of $1,000 and a savings rate of 10 percent. The household would then spend $900 and save $100. In a textbook world, the saved $100 is taken up by the financial sector and lent to the borrower who can make the best use of the money. When that borrower spends the $100, aggregate expenditure totals $1,000 ($900 plus $100) against an original income of $1,000, and the economy moves on. When there is insufficient credit demand for the $100 in savings, interest rates are lowered, which usually prompts a borrower to take up the remaining sum. When credit demand is excessive, interest rates are raised, prompting some borrowers to drop out.

By contrast, in a world where the private sector is minimizing its debt there are no borrowers for the saved $100 even at an interest rate of zero, leaving only $900 in expenditures. This $900 represents someone's income, and if the earners of that income also save 10 percent, only $810 will be spent. Since repairing balance sheets after a major asset bubble typically takes years—15 years in the case of Japan—the saved $90 will go unborrowed again, and the demand for goods and services will shrink to $810, in the next round to $730, and so on. This process will continue until the private sector either has repaired its balance sheet or become too poor to save (i.e., the economy enters a depression).

A deflationary spiral triggered by debt repayment is exactly what happened during America's Great Depression, which was a balance sheet recession in its purest form (i.e., one that was not mitigated by government intervention). The US private sector collectively rushed to pay down debt following the bursting of the debt-financed stock market bubble in October 1929. With existing borrowers reducing their debt and no one taking out new loans, the United States entered the kind of deflationary spiral described here, losing 46 percent of its GDP in the four years from 1929 to 1933.

Like the nationwide debt-financed bubbles that necessarily precede them, balance sheet recessions are very rare. But when they happen they can lead to a depression if not properly addressed.

The World in Balance Sheet Recession

In the United States, the United Kingdom, Spain, and Ireland (but not Greece) the private sector is undertaking massive deleveraging efforts in response to a collapse in housing prices in spite of record low interest rates. In other words, these countries are all in severe balance sheet recessions. Nor are businesses and households in Japan or Germany borrowing much. With private-sector borrowers disappearing everywhere, it is no wonder that these economies are still doing so poorly even though interest rates have been at record lows over nearly four years and central banks have made massive liquidity injections.

Flow-of-funds data for the United States show a massive shift away from borrowing to savings by the private sector since the housing bubble burst in 2007 (figure 4.1). The US private sector (household and corporate sectors) was a net borrower to the tune of 5 percent of GDP in 2007, but by 2010 it was saving a net 8 percent of GDP. In other words, the US economy lost private demand equivalent to 13 percent of GDP in the space of just three years. The fact that the private sector in the United States is now saving over 5 percent of GDP despite zero interest rates indicates that the US economy is in a full-blown balance sheet recession.

Flow-of-funds data for the United Kingdom tell a similar story, with its private sector squarely in financial surplus. The fact that

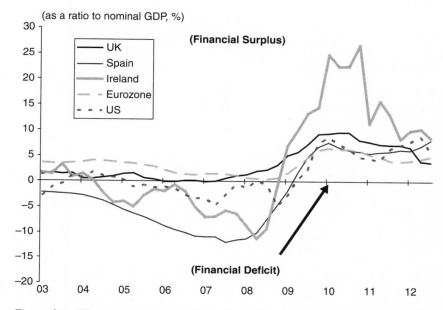

Figure 4.1 Western economies in balance sheet recessions: massive increases in private-sector savings after the bubble.

Notes: Private sector = household sector + nonfinancial corporate sector + financial sector. All entries are four-quarter moving averages. For the latest figures, four-quarter averages ending with 3Q/'12 are used.

Sources: Flow of funds data from Office for National Statistics, UK, Banco de España, National Statistics Institute, Spain, The Central Bank of Ireland, Central Statistics Office Ireland, ECB, Eurostat, FRB, and US Department of Commerce.

the sector is saving 3.8 percent of GDP in spite of the lowest interest rates in modern British history shows the UK economy is also in a balance sheet recession. The same pattern can be observed in the Euro zone since 2008. Japan, too, had fallen into a balance sheet recession after its bubble burst in 1990 (figure 4.2).

Japanese businesses had borrowed and invested some 12 percent of GDP during the bubble. But by 2003 they were paying down debt to the tune of 10 percent of GDP in response to a staggering 87 percent decline in nationwide commercial real estate values. In effect, corporate deleveraging caused a loss of domestic demand equivalent to 22 percent of GDP. This massive deleveraging lasted

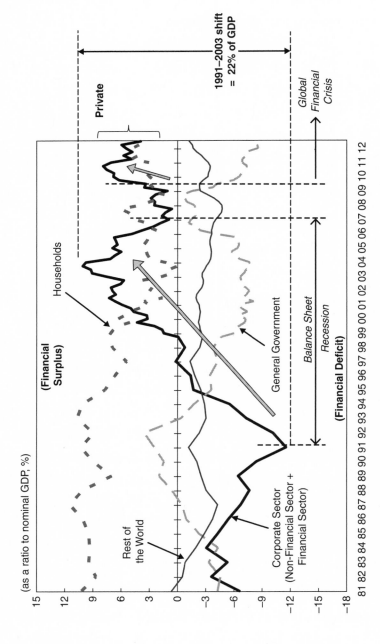

Figure 4.2   Balance sheet recession in Japan: renewed increase in corporate savings after the collapse of Lehman Brothers.

Note: All entries are four-quarter moving averages. For the latest figures, four-quarter averages ending with 3Q/'12 are used.

Sources: Bank of Japan, *Flow of Funds Accounts*, and Government of Japan, Cabinet Office, *National Accounts*.

until 2005 and resumed in 2008 with the global financial crisis, notwithstanding zero interest rates.

Historically it is not unusual for both the household and corporate sectors to run a financial surplus, especially when monetary authorities want to rein in the economy with higher interest rates. But the fact that this is happening at a time when interest rates are near zero makes the current situation both extremely unusual and worrisome. It is this very combination, after all, that led to Japan's "lost decade" in the 1990s.

Monetary Policy Loses Effectiveness When There Are No Borrowers

The first casualty of a shift toward debt minimization is monetary policy, the traditional remedy for recessions, because people with negative equity are not interested in increasing their borrowings at any interest rate. Nor will there be many willing lenders for those with impaired balance sheets, especially when the lenders themselves have balance sheet problems. And when the private sector is collectively drawing down bank deposits to repay debt, the money multiplier turns negative at the margin and the money supply, which consists mostly of bank deposits, contracts. Although the central bank can inject any amount of liquidity into the banking system, it will be hard-pressed to reverse a shrinkage of the money supply when there are no borrowers and the liquidity it provides cannot leave the banking system.

As shown in figure 4.3, massive injections of liquidity by both the Federal Reserve and the Bank of England since 2008 have failed to prevent contractions in credit available to the private sector in their respective countries. A more recent easing action by the European Central Bank (ECB) also resulted in minimal credit

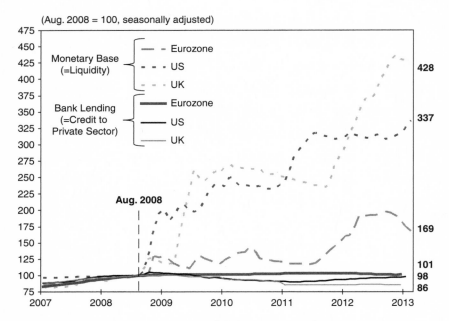

Figure 4.3 Massive quantitative easing failed to increase credit to private sector.

Notes: 1. The United Kingdom's reserve balances data are seasonally unadjusted.

2. The United Kingdom's bank lending data exclude intermediate financial institutions.

3. Base money's figures of Eurozone are seasonally adjusted by Nomura Research Institute.

Source: Nomura Research Institute, based on FRB, ECB, and Bank of England data.

expansion. In Japan, even a tripling of the monetary base by the Bank of Japan starting in 1990 failed to increase private-sector credit, which still remains at the level of 1990 (figure 4.4). The absence of credit growth despite record-low interest rates in all of these countries indicates that monetary policy has largely lost its effectiveness.

In all of these countries it has been argued that slow credit growth is attributable to bankers being saddled with bad debt, which is preventing them from lending. This "credit crunch" argument has been widely disseminated by the media because bankers who are not lending make an excellent target for editorialists as well as politicians.

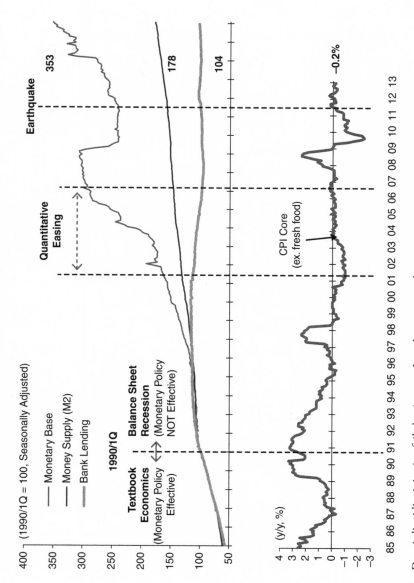

Figure 4.4 Drastic liquidity injection failed to increase Japan's money supply.

Note: Bank lending is seasonally adjusted by Nomura Research Institute.

Source: Bank of Japan.

However, the Bank of Japan has for decades been asking over 10,000 corporate borrowers how they perceive bankers' willingness to lend. Their answers, which form the Tankan Survey (figure 4.5), show that bankers were willing to lend except for three occasions in 1997, 2002, and 2008. Yet, it was the corporate sector that refused to borrow even at the lowest level of interest rates in history. This finding suggests that, contrary to popular perception, the lack of demand for funds has been a far bigger problem than a lack of supply.

A similar result had been obtained in a 1932 survey conducted by the National Industrial Conference Board at the behest of the US Congress in the midst of the Great Depression. This survey indicated that as much as 86 percent of the respondents had experienced no problems with their bankers, a result that at the time shocked the policymakers who had commissioned the survey, because it diverged greatly from the popular perception.

More importantly, the 14 percent answering that they *had* experienced problems were not sufficient to explain the 47 percent decline in bank lending during this period. This implies that most of the decline in lending was due to borrowers choosing to minimize debt rather than lenders calling in loans.

With existing borrowers repaying their debt and no one taking out new loans, the US money multiplier turned negative at the margin and the money supply shrunk by over 30 percent from 1929 to 1933. That prompted deflation in some quarters, which many have blamed for the prolonged weakness of the US economy in the 1930s. Those same commentators told Japan in the 1990s that its economy would recover quickly if the Bank of Japan only reflated the economy with more quantitative easing and an inflation target.

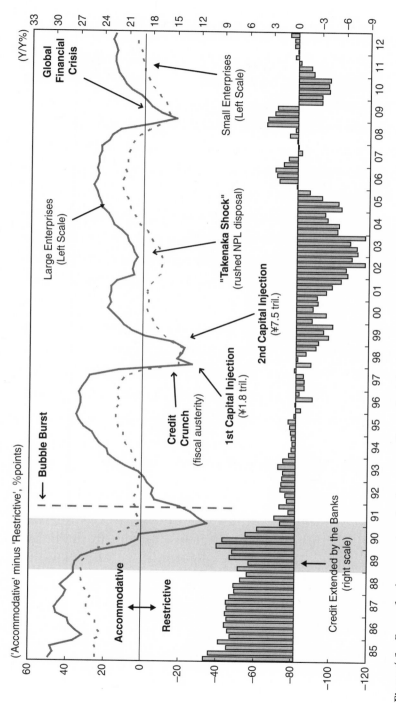

Figure 4.5 Except for three occasions, bankers were willing to lend, but borrowers refused to borrow.

Note: Shaded areas indicate periods of BOJ monetary tightning.

Sources: Bank of Japan, "Tankan," "Loans and Discounts Outstanding by Sector"

What they failed to notice was that people were paying down debt in response to a fall in *asset* prices, not consumer prices. Unless asset prices are brought back to bubble levels and kept there, a near-impossible task, there is no reason for the private sector to stop deleveraging even if consumer price inflation becomes positive.

Proof of this can be found in the fact that consumer price inflation of more than 2 percent in both the United States and the United Kingdom have failed to stop the deleveraging process in these countries even in an environment of negative real interest rates, and the two economies are performing no better than the Japanese economy with its zero inflation rate. This means that positive inflation rates and negative real interest rates are not enough to stop the private sector from deleveraging when it faces balance sheet problems.

It should also be noted that the money multiplier will remain negative at the margin as long as the deleveraging process continues in the private sector as a whole. Thus, the central bank is deprived of the means of generating the money supply growth needed to lift the inflation rate.

The Significance of Japan's Experience

Japan faced a balance sheet recession after 1990 as its asset price bubble burst and commercial real estate prices fell by 87 percent nationwide. The resulting loss of national wealth in shares and real estate alone amounted to 1,500 trillion yen, equivalent to three times 1989 GDP. In comparison, the United States during the Great Depression lost national wealth equivalent to just one year of 1929 GDP. Japan's corporate sector responded by shifting from its traditional role as a large borrower of funds to a massive repayer of debt, as indicated earlier.

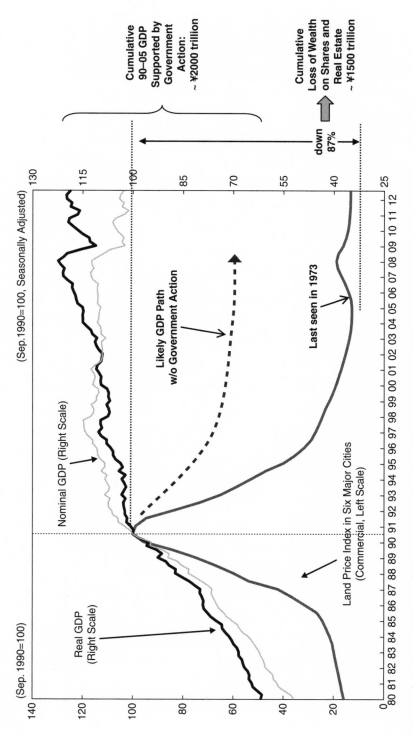

Figure 4.6 Japan: GDP growth despite massive loss of wealth and private-sector deleveraging.

Sources: Cabinet Office, Japan Real Estate Institute.

In spite of the tremendous loss of wealth and private-sector deleveraging, Japan managed to keep its GDP above bubble-peak levels throughout the post-1990 era (figure 4.6), and its unemployment rate never climbed above 5.5 percent. Japan was able to avoid a depression because the government borrowed and spent the additional savings (the $100 in the example given earlier) every year, thereby keeping the economy's expenditures at $1,000 ($900 in private sector spending plus $100 in government spending).

This government action supported incomes in the private sector and allowed businesses and households to continue to gradually repay their debt. By 2005 the private sector had completed its balance sheet repairs. With half of Japan's listed companies having effectively no debt at all (i.e., their financial assets exceed their financial liabilities), Japan probably has the world's cleanest corporate balance sheets today.

This fiscal action increased government debt by 460 trillion yen or 92 percent of GDP between 1990 and 2005, but the amount of GDP it preserved compared with a depression scenario was far greater. Under the rather optimistic assumption that without government action Japanese GDP would have returned to the prebubble level of 1985 (the dotted line in figure 4.6), the difference between this hypothetical level and actual GDP for the 15-year period would exceed 2,000 trillion yen. In effect, the Japanese government spent 460 trillion yen "to buy" 2,000 trillion yen of GDP, making it a tremendous bargain. And because the private sector was deleveraging at the same time, the government's fiscal action did not lead to crowding out, inflation, or skyrocketing interest rates.

Japan also managed to keep its money supply from shrinking during this period in spite of massive private-sector deleveraging because the government borrowed and spent excess private savings and prevented a contraction of banks' assets (figure 4.7).

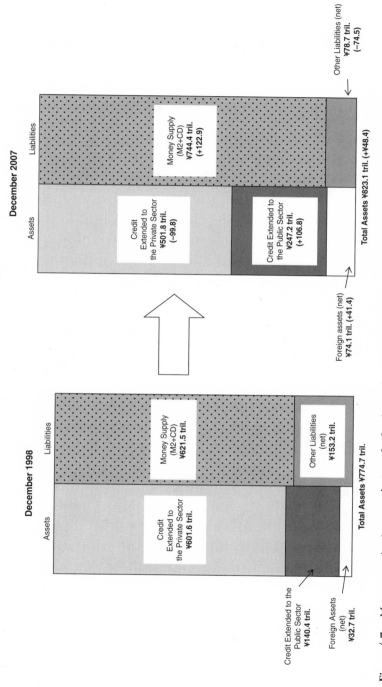

Balance Sheets of Banks in Japan

December 1998

Assets | Liabilities

Credit Extended to the Private Sector ¥601.6 tril.

Money Supply (M2+CD) ¥621.5 tril.

Credit Extended to the Public Sector ¥140.4 tril.

Foreign Assets (net) ¥32.7 tril.

Other Liabilities (net) ¥153.2 tril.

Total Assets ¥774.7 tril.

December 2007

Assets | Liabilities

Credit Extended to the Private Sector ¥501.8 tril. (−99.8)

Money Supply (M2+CD) ¥744.4 tril. (+122.9)

Credit Extended to the Public Sector ¥247.2 tril. (+106.8)

Foreign assets (net) ¥74.1 tril. (+41.4)

Other Liabilities (net) ¥78.7 tril. (−74.5)

Total Assets ¥823.1 tril. (+¥48.4)

Figure 4.7 Monetary easing is not a substitute for fiscal stimulus (I): Japan's money supply kept up by government borrowing.

Source: Bank of Japan "Monetary Survey."

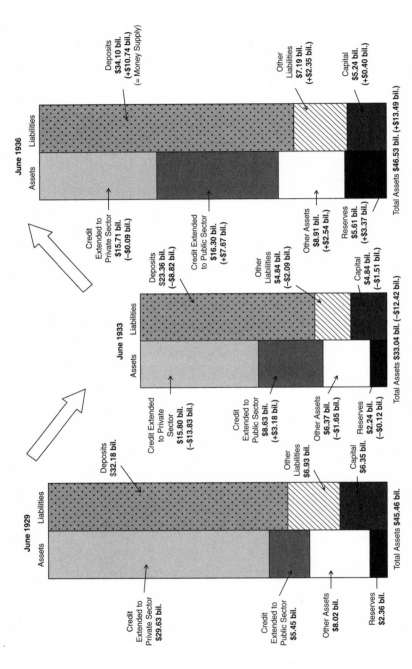

Figure 4.8 Monetary easing is not a substitute for fiscal stimulus (II): post-1933 US money supply growth made possible by government borrowing.

Source: Board of Governors of the Federal Reserve System (1976), *Banking and Monetary Statistics 1914–1941*, pp. 72–79.

This was similar to what had happened in the United States after 1933, when money supply growth resumed because the Roosevelt Administration borrowed aggressively to finance its New Deal programs, as shown in figure 4.8.

Balance Sheets of All Member Banks

Many authors over the last 30 years have argued that it was the change in monetary policy that led the United States to recover from the Great Depression, since the money supply, which represents a liability of the banking system, grew rapidly after 1933. But none of these authors bothered to look at the asset side of banks' balance sheets. From 1933 to 1936 the US money supply grew only because lending to the government increased, whereas lending to the private sector did not expand at all. The examples of the post-1990 Japanese and the post-1929 US experience indicate that fiscal stimulus is indispensible in keeping both GDP *and* the money supply from contracting during a balance sheet recession.

Unfortunately, the proponents of fiscal consolidation in the Western economies today are only looking at the size of fiscal deficits while ignoring the growth in private savings. Indeed, they are bound to repeat Japan's disastrous experiments with premature fiscal consolidation in 1997 and 2001, both of which triggered a deflationary spiral and ultimately *increased* the fiscal deficit (figure 4.9).

The 1997 austerity program, which raised taxes and cut spending at the urging of the IMF and other orthodox economists, led to five quarters of negative growth in Japan and increased its fiscal deficit by 68 percent, from 22 trillion yen in 1996 to 38 trillion yen in 1999. It took the country 10 years to get out of the hole created by this policy error. Japan would have emerged

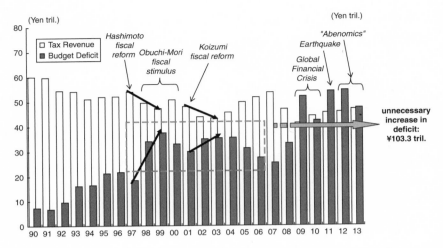

Figure 4.9 Japan: Premature Fiscal Reforms in 1997 and 2001—weakened economy, *reduced* tax revenue, and *increased* fiscal deficit.

Notes: Latest figures (*) are estimated by MOF. From FY2011, figures include reconstruction taxes and bonds.

Source: Ministry of Finance, Japan.

from its balance sheet recession much faster and at significantly lower cost than the 460 trillion yen noted earlier had the government not implemented austerity measures on those two occasions. The same mistake had been made in the United States in 1937, with equally devastating results.

Except for certain countries in the Euro zone, which will be discussed in detail here, there is no reason why a government should face financing problems during a balance sheet recession. This is because the amount of money it must borrow and spend to avert a deflationary spiral is equal to the amount of unborrowed and uninvested private savings (the $100 mentioned earlier) languishing somewhere in the country's financial system.

With the private sector as a whole no longer borrowing money, fund managers who must reinvest the debt repayments as well as new savings but are unable to assume too much principle risk (i.e., cannot put all their money in equities) or foreign exchange risk due to government regulations have no choice but to buy government bonds. This is why government bond yields drop to unusually low levels during a balance sheet recession.

The low yields on government bonds during such a recession are not a bubble: they are exactly what one would expect when the government becomes the last borrower standing. These low yields are also the market's message to policymakers that this is not the time to reduce the deficit. During a balance sheet recession fiscal stimulus not only prevents the economy and money supply from imploding, but also allows the government to carry out necessary public investment projects at the lowest possible cost to present and future taxpayers.

Nor is there any danger of misallocating resources or crowding out private-sector investments, because the government is simply borrowing and spending the unborrowed savings of the private sector. If the government failed to utilize those resources in order to provide a fiscal stimulus, they would simply go unemployed, which is the worst form of resource allocation.

Deficit hawks pushing for fiscal consolidation often talk about the "bond market vigilantes," but a large number of bond market participants in Japan, the United States, and the United Kingdom are already familiar with the concept of balance sheet recessions and use the term to describe what is happening to their economies. This is consistent with the fact that 10-year bond yields in these countries are hitting all-time lows in spite of record budget deficits. Indeed, bond market participants are usually the first to notice private-sector debt minimization because it is their job to reinvest rising private savings just when demand for funds from traditional private-sector borrowers is fading.

Reasons for the Euro Zone Debt Crisis

As fund managers in the United States, the United Kingdom, and Japan talk about balance sheet recessions and government bond yields in these countries have fallen to historic lows, bond yields in Euro zone countries such as Spain and Ireland remain high and in some cases are rising further. That has ignited concerns about a sovereign debt crisis and a breakup of the Euro zone, both of which could have devastating global consequences.

This phenomenon is rooted in a factor that is unique to the Euro zone. Unlike their counterparts elsewhere, Euro zone fund managers can buy bonds issued by other Euro zone governments without taking on any exchange-rate risk. If they are concerned about their own government's fiscal position, they can simply buy other Euro zone debt, leading to a unique kind of capital flight within government bond markets.

Spain and Ireland, for instance, are both in the midst of severe balance sheet recessions, with net private savings amounting to 8.1 percent and 8.6 percent of GDP, respectively (figure 4.1), in spite of record low interest rates. This means there is plenty of private savings available in these countries. However, many Spanish and Irish fund managers who do not like their own governments' debt are buying German government bonds instead.

My worst fears were confirmed on a trip to Madrid in November 2011 when I found that every fund manager attending my seminar was moving funds out of Spain to Germany. Such capital flight not only leaves the governments of both Spain and Ireland unable to tap the private savings surpluses in their own country to fight the balance sheet recession, but also forces them to carry out austerity programs as bond yields go up rather than down. This causes the aforementioned $100 to drop out of the income stream, prompting a deflationary spiral. In effect, they are forced into repeating the Japanese mistake of 1997. The resulting deflationary spiral scares investors even more and prompts them to move even more funds abroad in a vicious cycle. It is therefore no surprise that Spanish bond yields are so high and that the nation's unemployment rate has been rising rapidly.

The Japanese meltdown in 1997 ignited a massive banking crisis and credit crunch, as shown in figure 4.5. Japanese banks that had endured the shock of a burst bubble for six full years were unable to cope with the austerity-triggered double-dip in 1997. A similar pattern can now be observed in Spain, where banks were able to withstand the initial global financial shock well but were subsequently hit by an austerity-led deflationary cycle that pushed the unemployment rate from 12.3 percent at the time of Lehman's collapse to 26.1 percent today.

If countries, like Germany, that are at the receiving end of the capital flight actively borrowed and spent the money flowing in from Spain and Ireland, this would sustain economic activity in the broader Euro zone and would probably have positive repercussions on Spain and Ireland as well. But with unemployment in Germany at a 20-year low, the government sees no need for additional fiscal stimulus and is leading an effort to enforce compliance with the 3-percent deficit ceiling specified in the Maastricht Treaty. However, if the Spanish savings fleeing to Germany are not borrowed and spent, the result will be an economic contraction throughout the Euro zone.

Until just a few years ago, capital flows within the Euro zone were following the opposite pattern. Banks in Germany, which had fallen into a balance sheet recession after the country's telecom bubble collapsed in 2000, aggressively bought bonds issued by southern European governments because they were denominated in the same currency but offered higher yields than domestic offerings. The resulting capital inflows from Germany poured further fuel onto the fire of housing bubbles in these countries (a point discussed further later). But once the bubbles collapsed, the capital flows reversed, sparking capital flight.

The problem with these abrupt shifts in capital flows is that they are highly procyclical and destabilizing. Countries that are in the midst of bubbles are receiving massive inflows although they do not need, or want, additional funds. Meanwhile, countries that are facing balance sheet recessions and desperately in need of funds can only watch domestic and foreign savings flowing abroad, unable to implement the fiscal stimulus needed to stabilize their economies.

A Solution for the Euro Zone: Allow Only Nationals to Buy Domestic Government Bonds

One way to resolve this crisis would be to announce that, after a transition period of perhaps five–ten years, member governments will replace the 3-percent deficit rule with a new rule prohibiting the sale of government bonds to foreigners. For example, Greece would be permitted to sell its government debt only to Greek nationals.

Such a rule would enable national governments to achieve both fiscal discipline and fiscal flexibility and prevent a repetition of today's problems. It would restore fiscal discipline because governments would not be able to run larger deficits than what their citizens can tolerate. It would also provide fiscal flexibility by allowing governments to run deficits larger than 3 percent of GDP if they can convince citizens that those deficits are necessary. This is of critical importance during a balance sheet recession, when a larger deficit may be necessary to stabilize the economy.

Most importantly, this rule would keep destabilizing capital flows in check. For example, it would prevent Spanish savings from fleeing into German government bonds, since Spanish citizens would no longer be allowed to purchase those bonds. Indeed, the whole point of this rule is to put Euro zone fund managers on an equal footing with fund managers elsewhere, thereby containing destabilizing flows between government bond markets. Given the large surplus of private savings in Spain, that alone would bring Spanish government bond yields down to levels comparable to those in countries outside the Euro zone, like the United Kingdom and the United States. No one would be talking about a Spanish sovereign debt crisis if the nation's bond yields were at historic lows. The same is true of Ireland.

This rule would also prevent fiscal problems and political changes in one nation from threatening the broader currency area by making fiscal policy an *internal* issue for individual countries. If the Greek government were to default, for example, it would be a problem only for the Greek public and could be considered separately from the health of the Euro zone as a whole. This would also free the ECB from having to worry about the fiscal health of member governments and allow it to concentrate on managing monetary policy.

Moreover, this rule would change the tenor of the national political debate. Protesters in the streets of various capitals could no longer blame everything on bureaucrats in Brussels, bankers in Paris, or politicians in Berlin. Instead, they would have to redirect their energies to persuading their relatives and friends to buy more of their own government's debt.

Although this rule would constitute a kind of capital control, limiting the sale of government bonds to citizens represents a *minimal* constraint on the free movement of capital. Euro zone citizens would still be able to buy private-sector assets of other member countries, which is where the efficiency gains from a single currency really matter. Indeed, it is difficult to see what kind of efficiency gain is obtained by allowing German banks to buy Greek government bonds. On the contrary, German bank purchases of Greek government bonds allowed the latter to run an ever more profligate fiscal policy, which, in the end, resulted in diminished economic gains for everyone. Since government bonds always offer the lowest yields in the capital market, the inability to buy another member nation's bonds will not be a great loss to Euro zone residents.

For an integrated financial market such as Europe, making capital controls watertight would not be easy, even with the harshest of penalties. But if enough investors abide by the rule, Spanish and Irish bond yields would come down substantially, helping not only those countries but also the investors who observed the rule. For the purpose of this rule, financial institutions that are supervised domestically should be considered national institutions, so that the authorities can ensure they are not buying government bonds on behalf of nonnationals.

The proposed rule would also ensure fiscal sovereignty for individual countries, instead of subjugating them to the whims of bureaucrats in Brussels or politicians in Berlin. Indeed, the challenge for democracy in the Euro zone today is how to make citizens feel they are empowered to decide their own destiny without jeopardizing the credibility of the Euro as a common currency. A rule limiting the issuance of government bonds to citizens of the issuing nation would address this challenge by giving member governments complete freedom of fiscal policy as long as they do not sell their bonds to nonnationals.

Artificial constraints are required to maintain an artificial currency area like the Euro zone. The Maastricht Treaty's cap on fiscal deficits at 3 percent of GDP represented a first attempt at such a constraint. But the current crisis has made it clear that it is incapable of addressing destabilizing capital flows or balance sheet recessions.

Spain's private sector, for example, is saving over 8 percent of GDP today even though interest rates are close to zero. If the Spanish government is allowed to borrow only 3 percent of GDP, the remaining 5 percent will leak out of the income stream and the Spanish economy will shrink by 5 percent per year. But the treaty says nothing about this kind of predicament because conventional economics never anticipated a private sector saving so much at such a low level of interest rates. Replacing the 3-percent cap with a rule prohibiting the sale of government bonds to foreigners would restore fiscal discipline in these countries and enable authorities to respond appropriately to balance sheet recessions.

In retrospect, this rule should have been in place since the beginning of the Euro. None of the problems the Euro zone now faces would have occurred if that were the case. Unfortunately, the Euro was allowed to continue for more than ten years without the rule, leading to the accumulation of massive imbalances. Since it will probably take many years to undo the damage, a transition period is needed.

During the transition period, it may be useful to introduce different risk weights for domestic and nondomestic government bonds held by banks and institutional investors in the Euro zone. In this scheme, domestic government bonds should carry a lower risk weight than nondomestic government bonds. The logic here is that domestic investors should be better able to assess their own government and the quality of the bonds issued by that government. If such a rule encourages enough funds to stay at home, some of the instability and tensions in the Euro zone capital market today may well dissipate. Since such risk weights will not be considered a "capital control," it may be easier politically to implement as well.

In order to lift the Euro zone out of the crisis a two-pronged approach is required. For Ireland, Spain, and other countries in balance sheet recessions, the EU and the ECB should announce a new diagnosis. They should acknowledge that massive private-sector deleveraging at a time of record low interest rates has plunged these countries into balance sheet recessions, forcing them to administer fiscal stimuli in order to stabilize their economies. They should also make it clear that they stand ready to help. Such support from supranational institutions is absolutely essential because in its absence capital flight will only accelerate. The afflicted countries, meanwhile, should proceed with fiscal consolidation only when their private sectors have restored their balance sheets and are ready to borrow again.

For Greece, which is not in a balance sheet recession, fiscal austerity is essential. It will also need bridge financing until its government can run on domestic savings alone.

Moreover, Euro zone member states should make a joint declaration to the effect that in ten years they will stop selling government debt to nonnationals. If such a move proves to be difficult politically, the governments should introduce different risk weights for holdings of domestic verses foreign government bonds in order to rein in destabilizing capital flights. This commitment to an endgame is needed to assure lenders and taxpayers in creditor countries—whose help will be needed during the short-run—that the present problems will not be repeated. Once investors are assured that this austerity-fueled vicious cycle will be arrested and the endgame is credible, they may well find current Euro zone bond yields attractive.

The Post-2000 German Balance Sheet Recession and the "Competitiveness Problem"

Many in Europe continue to insist that southern European countries should leave the Euro zone and return to their own (weaker) currencies because their economies are uncompetitive. While the large trade deficits in these countries would seem to support this argument, there is a problem with the assumption underlying it, namely that the loss of competitiveness is only the result of poor domestic policy choices.

If a country is experiencing inflation and its monetary authorities do not tighten policy, wages will rise and the international competitiveness of their producers will suffer. The country then needs to restore competitiveness by devaluing the currency, something that happened frequently in southern Europe in the pre-Euro era. But within the Euro zone there is no way for one country to tighten monetary policy unilaterally as all Euro zone countries are operating under the same monetary policy determined by the ECB. That begs the question of why such a large gap in competitiveness among the members of the zone could develop in the first place.

The Germans' answer is that they regained competitiveness through painful structural reforms aimed at improving labor market flexibility and bolstering the pension system during the 2000s. Indeed, their position has been that until peripheral countries implement similar structural reforms, they will not be offering financial assistance to those countries. The tripartite agreement in 1999 between labor, employers, and the government to keep wage growth below productivity growth also contributed to the improvement in German competitiveness in no small way (as pointed out by Heiner Flassbeck in this volume).

However, although these arrangements made a big difference for German competitiveness, they were by no means the only factor: money supply (M3) growth in Germany and other countries

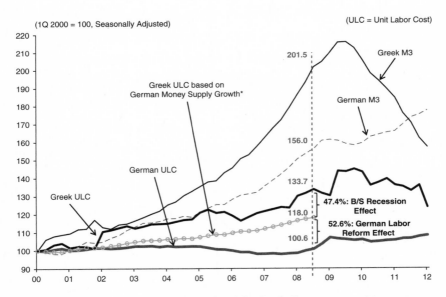

Figure 4.10 Micro and macro factors behind the Greek-German competitiveness gap.

Note: *Parameters obtained from the regression result on Greek ULC on Greek M3, log(Greek ULC) = 2.92075 + log(Greek M3) x 0.372586, applied to German M3 data indexed to 1Q 2000 = 100.

Sources: Nomura Research Institute, based on ECB, Deutsche Bundesbank, and Bank of Greece data.

in the Euro zone also diverged significantly during the same period. As figure 4.10 shows, the German money supply grew by 56 percent from the first quarter 2000 to the third quarter 2008. Over the same time span, the Greek money supply increased by 102 percent. This differential of 46 percentage points naturally led to significant disparities in price competitiveness between the two countries. (Money supply growth in the Euro zone excluding Germany was 109 percent during this period.)

During the same period, Greek unit labor cost increased 33.7 percent while German unit labor cost rose by only 0.6 percent. If we apply the parameters obtained from regressing the Greek unit labor cost on Greek money supply to the German money supply growth, the German unit labor cost should have increased by 18.0 percent during that period. In other words, if the Germans had operated just like the Greeks and implemented no structural reforms or wage restraint, slower money supply growth in Germany would have explained 15.7 percentage points out of 33.1 percentage points (or 47 percent) of the differential in unit labor cost between the two countries in the third quarter 2008. This also suggests that the wage restraint noted by Heiner Flassbeck and other structural reforms in Germany accounted for the remaining 53 percent of the gap—as depicted in figure 4.10.

The disparity in money supply growth can be traced to the collapse of the German telecom bubble in 2000, which plunged the country into a severe balance sheet recession. The *Neue Markt*, essentially a German version of Nasdaq, plunged 96 percent from its peak and eventually had to be shut down. Private-sector balance sheets were hit hard, prompting German households and businesses to sharply increase savings and debt repayment starting in 2000 (figure 4.11). The shift in German household sector behavior after 2000 was nothing short of dramatic: it stopped

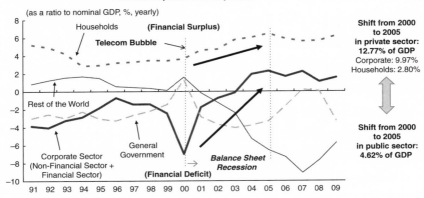

Figure 4.11 Germany: balance sheet recession after the 1999–2000 telecom bubble.

Note: The assumption of Treuhand agency's debt by the Redemption Fund for Inherited Liabilities in 1995 is adjusted.

Sources: Deutsche Bundesbank, Federal Statistical Office Germany.

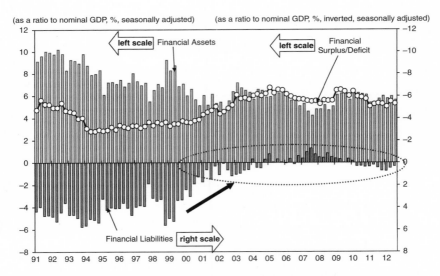

Figure 4.12 German households stopped borrowing money after IT bubble.

Note: Seasonal adjustments by Nomura Research Institute. Latest figures are for 2012 Q3.

Sources: Nomura Research Institute, based on flow of funds data from Bundesbank and Eurostat.

borrowing money altogether, as shown in figure 4.12. This shift from profit maximization to debt minimization in the private sector amounted to 12.1 percent of German GDP from 2000 to 2005, slashing domestic demand and throwing the economy into a deep recession.

We have already seen that monetary policy becomes impotent when the private sector is minimizing debt. Fiscal stimulus was therefore needed to support the German economy. But Germany was unable to mobilize fiscal policy sufficiently because of the cap on fiscal deficits agreed in the Maastricht Treaty. Germany's actual fiscal deficits modestly exceeded the 3-percent threshold on several occasions, but the resulting fiscal stimulus was far from being sufficient to prop up the economy.

In a bid to rescue the Euro zone's largest economy, the ECB then lowered its policy rate from 4.75 percent in 2001 to a post-war low of 2 percent in 2003. But the ultralow rates had little impact on Germany, where balance sheet problems were forcing businesses and households to minimize debt. The money supply grew very slowly, and with German households not borrowing money at all, the German house price index actually *fell* from 100 in 2000 to 92 in 2005, although interest rates had reached a postwar low. Naturally, there was only minimal inflation in wages or prices.

The countries of southern Europe, which had not participated in the IT bubble, were enjoying an economic boom and robust private-sector demand for funds. The ECB's policy rate of 2 percent therefore led to rapid growth in credit and the money supply, which in turn fueled not only economic growth, but also real-estate bubbles. In Spain, for example, the house price index shot up from 100 in 2000 to 207 in 2005. The index rose to 176 in

Ireland and to 166 in Greece over the same period. Wages and prices increased rapidly as well, leaving those countries less competitive relative to Germany.

In short, the ECB's ultralow policy rate had little impact in Germany, which was suffering from a balance sheet recession, but it was too accommodative for other economies in the Euro zone. The result was widely divergent rates of inflation.

The fact that German household and corporate sectors were not only refraining from borrowing, but were saving as much as 8 percent of GDP by 2004, as shown in figure 4.11, and the fact that the German government was constrained from running a budget deficit larger than 3 percent of GDP meant that German financial institutions had no choice but to lend the difference to borrowers abroad. This led to capital outflows from Germany, which contributed to the bubbles in the peripheral countries, as mentioned earlier. Some of the outflows also helped finance the housing bubble in the United States as German banks purchased a considerable amount of subprime papers.

With German producers becoming increasingly competitive relative to those in the booming economies of southern Europe, German exports grew sharply, pulling the nation out of recession. While Germany overtook Japan and China to post the world's largest trade surplus, the growth in the trade surplus was driven mainly by exports to other European countries rather than Asia or North America (figure 4.13). This suggests that it was primarily the intra-European inflation differential that gave Germany such a large competitive advantage. In other words, if the ECB had not inflated other Euro-zone economies to the extent it did, the German trade surplus would have been much smaller.

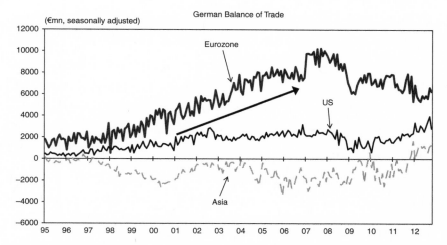

Figure 4.13 Germany: post telecom-bubble recovery led by exports to the Euro zone.
Source: Deutsche Bundesbank.

More importantly, there would have been no need for such dramatic easing by the ECB from 2000 to 2005—hence, no reason for the competitiveness gap to widen to current levels—if the German government had provided fiscal stimulus to address the post-2000 balance sheet recession. German banks would have also purchased fewer bonds of peripheral countries and fewer US subprime papers if they had been able to buy more government bonds at home. Unfortunately, the creators of the Maastricht Treaty failed to make provisions for balance sheet recessions when drawing up the document. Indeed, a significant part of today's "competitiveness problem" is attributable to the treaty's 3-percent cap on fiscal deficits, which places unreasonable demands on ECB monetary policy during this type of recession.

The Greek government is clearly to blame for the profligate fiscal policy of the past. But the competitiveness gap Greece and other southern European economies now labor under is not the fault of their governments.

Spain and Ireland are now experiencing severe balance sheet recessions, with a further deceleration of money supply growth likely to weigh on prices and wages. The Greek money supply is already shrinking rapidly as funds flee the country. The German economy, on the other hand, has emerged from the post-2000 balance sheet recession and is firing on all cylinders. Yet, the ECB has brought its policy rate down to 0.75 percent in an attempt to boost those economies that are in deep crisis.

However, the 0.75-percent policy rate will do little to help Spain and Ireland, because these countries are in balance sheet recessions. At the same time, this policy rate, together with yields of less than 1.5 percent of 10-year German government bonds, is clearly too low for Germany's booming economy and has already prompted the first surge in house prices in more than 15 years. The fact that German households are finally borrowing money and buying homes suggests that money supply growth is likely to accelerate. German prices and wages are also likely to rise further.

This means we are now witnessing the exact opposite of the events following the collapse of the IT bubble, when the economies of southern Europe were healthy and Germany was limping. Eventually, the paths of money supply growth and labor costs in Germany (increasing) and the rest of the Euro zone (decelerating or decreasing) will cross, eliminating the competitiveness gap between the two.

Figure 4.14 plots the trends in unit labor costs over the past two years and extends them into the future. The trend lines suggest that unit labor costs in Germany, on the one hand, and in Spain, Ireland, Greece, and Portugal, on the other, will cross paths between 2015 and 2017. Developments of the last 12 months

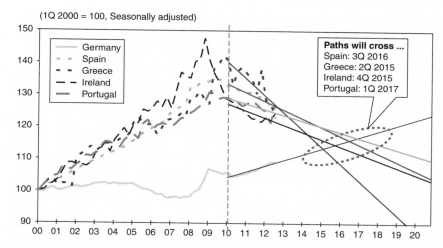

Figure 4.14 Expected convergence of unit labor costs in the Euro zone.

Notes: The figures of Greece are seasonally adjusted by Nomura Research Institute. Path of ULC growth was estimated based on trend from 1Q 2010 to 3Q 2012.

Source: Nomura Research Institute, based on ECB's data.

suggest that their paths may actually cross much sooner than that. Money supply growth in Greece has already fallen below that of Germany, and even some Germans are noting that Greek wages and prices are becoming more competitive.

There is no reason for Greece to leave the Euro zone for competitiveness reasons if Greek wages and prices will regain competitiveness within the next two or three years. This is because a recovery from the shock of an exit from the Euro could easily take five–ten years, if the post-2001 Argentinean experience is any guide. If labor unions in countries with high unemployment like Spain and Greece were to accept wage cuts in exchange for job security, the competitiveness problem could resolve itself even sooner. If the Germans also allow their wages to go up in line with productivity increases, as urged by Heiner Flassbeck in this volume, the adjustment time will be reduced even further.

Such gyrations between internal deflation (as in Germany from 2000 and in southern Europe and Ireland from 2008) and internal inflation (as in southern Europe and Ireland from 2000 and in Germany from 2010) are far from ideal. These macro-level divergences and fluctuations will plague the Euro zone as long as some member countries are in balance sheet recessions and others are not. The only way to eradicate the problem is to require those countries that are in balance sheet recessions to provide the necessary fiscal stimulus that is needed in order to avoid the ECB's monetary policy being unduly distorted in an attempt to address these recessions.

Unfortunately, many European policymakers are still unaware of the economic disease called balance sheet recession. Their calls for greater fiscal austerity and a stronger fiscal union are not helpful in this regard because they would impose the same fiscal policy regime on all countries, whether they were in a balance sheet recession or not. Many Europeans have also written-off fiscal stimulus entirely because of the problems they face in government bond markets and the restrictions imposed by the Maastricht Treaty.

But until policymakers explain to the people that they face a different kind of disease requiring a different kind of treatment, the situation in Europe is likely to worsen further as both private *and* public sectors deleverage at the same time. Nothing is more likely to spark a vicious cycle than fiscal consolidation during a balance sheet recession. Once a different diagnosis and endgame are offered, assuring the market that current problems will not be repeated, bond investor interest is likely to revive because they can be sure that the vicious cycle has finally been brought to an end.

The Difficulty of Maintaining Fiscal Stimulus in a Democracy

In the United States, Federal Reserve chairman Ben Bernanke understands the risks posed by balance sheet recessions. He has been warning since early 2010 that now is not the time to engage in fiscal consolidation. This was underscored in his answer to a question at a press conference on April 25, 2012, regarding the Fed's response if Congress did not act to avoid the so-called fiscal cliff. He replied: "The size of the fiscal cliff is such that there is absolutely no chance that the Federal Reserve could or would have any ability whatsoever to offset that effect on the economy," thus acknowledging that monetary easing is no substitute for fiscal stimulus in the current recession.

In the United Kingdom, where the largest round of quantitative easing in history not only failed to produce the forecasted economic recovery but was even unable to prevent a double-dip recession, many policymakers and commentators are now using the term "balance sheet recession" to describe their economy's predicament.

Unfortunately, policymakers in both the United States and the United Kingdom have not widely articulated their knowledge and concerns to the general public, who still cannot understand why a government should be allowed to run a deficit when households and businesses are not. Consequently, many ordinary citizens in both countries still favor fiscal consolidation over fiscal stimulus in accordance with what they were taught in the past. The same is true for Japan.

More broadly, the post-2010 push for fiscal consolidation in all of these countries has proven again that it is extremely difficult to maintain fiscal stimulus in a democracy during peacetime. This is a crucial problem during a balance sheet recession, because fiscal stimulus must be maintained for the duration of the private-sector deleveraging process in order to minimize both the length and the final fiscal cost of the recession. In most democracies, unfortunately, fiscal hawks are out in numbers demanding an end to fiscal stimulus as soon as the economy shows the first signs of a revival.

As a result of this kind of backlash, the fiscal stimuli implemented in 2009 in response to the global financial crisis are being allowed to expire. Private-sector deleveraging, on the other hand, continues unabated at alarmingly high levels in all of these economies, which are therefore decelerating if not contracting.

If the contraction appears serious and painful enough, governments are likely to administer another round of fiscal stimulus, only to be forced back into fiscal consolidation once the stimulus breathes life back into the economy. Owing to this pattern of on-off-again stimulus, it took Japan 15 years to overcome its own balance sheet recession. Figure 4.9 shows that this policy zigzag, and especially the austerity initiatives of 1997 and 2001, prolonged Japan's recession by at least five years and unnecessarily added at least $1 trillion to the public debt. The same policy error led to the disastrous collapse of the US economy in 1937. Only during wartime, when both the need for government spending and the type of spending required are obvious to everyone, can democracies implement and sustain the kind of fiscal stimulus needed to overcome a balance sheet recession in the shortest possible time.

Even those governments that manage to prevent an economic meltdown by providing necessary fiscal stimulus *before* the crisis are likely to be condemned rather than praised by the public. This is because people are not taught about the specific nature of balance sheet recessions and typically cannot envision what might have happened in the absence of fiscal stimulus. Seeing only a large deficit and no crisis, they assume the money must have been wasted on useless projects.

This is why Japan's Liberal Democratic Party lost power in 2009, and how former prime minister Gordon Brown was defeated in the United Kingdom in 2010. This is also why President Barack Obama's Democrats were pummeled in the midterm elections in the United States in 2010. Although their actions saved their economies from devastating deflationary spirals after the collapse of the investment bank Lehmann Brothers, they were attacked by a public unable to contemplate the counterfactual scenario. Those who prevent a crisis never become heroes. Hollywood movies teach us that there can be no hero without a crisis.

It has also become popular in some circles to talk about the need for medium-term fiscal consolidation while at the same time advocating short-term fiscal stimulus. Although this sounds responsible at one level, it is totally irresponsible at another. When the private sector is deleveraging in spite of zero interest rates—a state of affairs that was never anticipated in the economics or business literature—it is safe to assume that the financial health of the private sector is seriously impaired. Talking about medium-term fiscal consolidation in this environment is like asking a seriously injured person just admitted to a hospital whether she can afford the expensive treatment she needs. If asked this question often enough, the patient may become so depressed and discouraged that her condition will actually worsen, ultimately resulting in an even larger medical bill.

It has also become commonplace to talk about the so-called policy duration effect of monetary policy. The July 2011 announcement by the Fed that it will not raise interest rates until well into 2013 (later extended to 2015) was a prime example of how to maximize this effect. Yet, for some reason no one talks about the policy duration effect of *fiscal* policy. Any discussion of medium-term fiscal consolidation effectively *minimizes* the policy duration effect of whatever fiscal stimulus is in place if businesses and households feel that their balance sheets will not be repaired within that time frame.

With so little historical data on how much time is needed to repair private-sector balance sheets in this type of recession, government forecasts are likely to turn out to be grossly optimistic. For example, even though the fiscal stimuli enacted by President Obama were absolutely essential, his promise early in his term to cut the deficit in half by the end of his four-year term was counterproductive at best, as subsequent events have demonstrated.

Since letting the "patient" die is not an option, the government must work to maximize the policy duration effect of both monetary and fiscal policies in order to minimize the final cost of treatment. It is never a good idea to step on both the brake pedal and the accelerator at the same time.

The "Exit Problem" in Balance Sheet Recessions

The long time required to pull out of a balance sheet recession in a democracy means that the private sector needs many painful years paying down debt from a stagnant or falling income. Such an experience is likely to bring about a debt-induced trauma that prevents the private sector from borrowing money even after balance sheets have been cleaned up. This trauma may take years, if not decades, to overcome. But until the private sector is both willing and able to borrow again, the economy will be operating at less than full potential and may require continued fiscal support from the government to stay afloat. Overcoming this aversion to debt may be called the "exit problem" of balance sheet recessions.

In Japan, where the private sector became extremely averse to borrowing after the bitter experience of paying down debt from 1990 to 2005, businesses refuse to borrow money although there are willing lenders and interest rates are at their lowest level in history. As figure 4.2 shows, Japan's private sector is saving 10 percent of GDP at zero interest rates, equaling the record set at the trough of the balance sheet recession in 2003. The 10-year government bond is therefore yielding less than 1 percent even though the national debt exceeds 200 percent of GDP.

In the United States, the private sector's devastating experience of paying down debt during the Great Depression resulted in such a deep aversion toward borrowing that interest rates remained low for 30 years, until 1959 (figure 4.15). The fact that it took

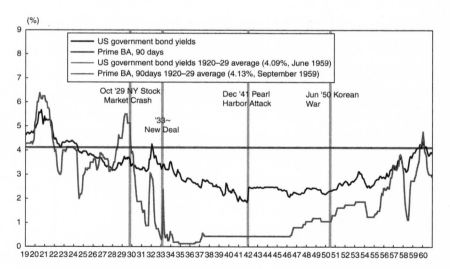

Figure 4.15 The exit problem: the United States took 30 years to normalize interest rates after 1929 because of private-sector aversion to debt.

Source: FRB, *Banking and Monetary Statistics 1914-1970 Vol.1*, pp. 450–451 and 468–471, vol. 2, pp. 674–676 and 720–727.

the United States three decades to bring interest rates back up to 4.1 percent, even with the massive fiscal stimulus of the New Deal and mobilization for World War II, underscores the severity of the trauma. One may even postulate that, had the Japanese not attacked Pearl Harbor, it would have taken the United States even more than these 30 years to return to a normal level of interest rates. Indeed, many Americans who were forced to pay down debt during the Depression never borrowed money again.

The experiences of the United States after 1929 and Japan after 1990 suggest that interest rates will remain low for a very long time even after private-sector balance sheets are repaired. Governments of countries facing exit problems should therefore introduce incentives for the nonfinancial corporate sector to borrow. Such incentives, which may include investment tax credits and accelerated depreciation allowances, should be exceptionally generous in order to attract sufficient private-sector participation. The sooner the trauma is overcome, the sooner the government can embark on fiscal consolidation. The initial generosity will more than pay for itself once this aversion to borrowing is overcome.

In any case, fiscal consolidation is not an option until the private sector is ready to borrow money again, as demonstrated in Japan in 1997 and the United States in 1937. All policy efforts should therefore be directed toward pulling economies out of balance sheet recessions in the shortest possible time. This means implementing substantial and sustained fiscal stimulus until private-sector balance sheets are repaired, followed by generous incentives for businesses to resume borrowing. Insufficient provision of fiscal stimulus because of concerns over the size of the deficit is a waste of time and resources, because it will only lengthen the recession and increase the final fiscal bill for treating this unusual disease.

There will be plenty of time to pay down the accumulated public debt because the next balance sheet recession of this magnitude is likely to be generations away. After all, those who learned a bitter lesson in the present episode will not make the same mistake again. A bubble and balance sheet recession of this magnitude will happen again only after those of us who remember the recent events are no longer around.

Distinguishing between Lender-Side and Borrower-Side Problems

It is also important to distinguish between balance sheet recessions and financial crises, since both are typically present in the years following the burst of a speculative bubble. The former concerns borrowers, while the latter concerns lenders. The distinction is important because the two require different policy responses. While monetary policy is largely impotent in a balance sheet recession, it can and must be fully mobilized to address financial crises. Available tools include liquidity infusions, capital injections, explicit and implicit guarantees, lower interest rates, and asset purchases.

The collapse of Lehman Brothers sparked a global financial crisis because of the mistaken decision by the US government not to safeguard the liabilities of a major financial institution when all other financial institutions faced similar problems. The resulting global panic weakened the economy far more severely and rapidly than what would have been suggested by balance sheet problems alone. This is why the panic subsided when the authorities moved to safeguard those liabilities. According to IMF figures, the Federal Reserve, together with governments and central banks around the world, injected some $8.9 trillion in liquidity and guarantees for this purpose in the wake of the Lehman failure. A large part of the recovery in share prices and industrial production observed in some quarters starting in the spring of 2009 was actually a recovery from the financial crisis, not from the balance sheet recession.

The financial panic has now subsided, but all the balance sheet problems that existed before Lehman Brothers failed are still in place. If anything, the steady fall in house prices since then has exacerbated those problems. And it is the balance sheet problems that are weighing on Western economies today. Recovering from the financial crisis was the easy part; the hard work of repairing millions of impaired private-sector balance sheets is just beginning.

The longer-term refinancing operations carried out by the ECB in December 2011 and February 2012 ("LTRO I and II") gave a huge boost to European banks. Because most European banks simultaneously faced the same problem, there was a great deal of mutual distrust, just as there had been in the United States following the Lehman collapse. The ECB's provision of liquidity via the LTROs was absolutely essential to avoid an implosion of the European banking system. However, these monetary actions failed to increase the money supply or bring about a turnaround in the European economies, because these also suffered from the borrower's problem—that is, a balance sheet recession—in addition to the problem of capital flight noted earlier.

Conclusion

It is laudable for policymakers to shun fiscal profligacy and to aim for self-reliance in the private sector. But every several decades, the private sector loses its self-control in a bubble and sustains critical financial injuries when the bubble bursts. That forces businesses and households to begin paying down debt in spite of zero interest rates, triggering a deflationary spiral. At such times, and at such times *only*, the government must borrow and spend the private sector's excess savings, not only to support output growth and to prevent an implosion of the money supply, but also to provide additional income to the private sector. The latter is required in order to allow the private sector to repair its balance sheets.

Anyone with political influence can push for fiscal consolidation in the form of higher taxes and lower spending. But whether such efforts actually succeed in reducing the budget deficit is an entirely different matter. When the private sector is both willing and able to borrow, fiscal consolidation will lead to smaller deficits and higher growth as resources are released to the more efficient private sector. But when the financial health of the private sector is so impaired that it is forced to deleverage even with interest rates at zero, a premature withdrawal of fiscal stimulus will widen the deficit and weaken the economy. Key differences between the textbook world and the world of balance sheet recessions are summarized in table 4.1.

With extensive private-sector deleveraging continuing on both sides of the Atlantic in spite of historically low interest rates, this is not the appropriate time to embark on fiscal consolidation. Such measures must wait until it is certain that the private sector has finished deleveraging and is ready to borrow again.

Up to now, the economics profession has assumed implicitly that there is only one type of recession and that depression is just an extreme form of recession. The Japanese experience from 1990 onward and the experience in the Western economies since 2008 indicate that there are actually two types of recession—one

Table 4.1 Textbook economics and balance sheet recession

		Textbook Economy	*Balance Sheet Recession*
1) Fundamental driver		Adam Smith's "invisible hand"	Fallacy of composition
2) Corporate financial condition		Assets > Liabilities	Assets < Liabilities
3) Behavioral principle		Profit maximization	Debt minimization
4) Outcome		Greatest good for greatest number	Depression if left unattended
5) Monetary policy		Effective	Ineffective (liquidity trap)
6) Fiscal policy		Counterproductive (crowding-out)	Effective
7) Prices		Inflationary	Deflationary
8) Interest rates		Normal	Very low
9) Savings		Virtue	Vice (paradox of thrift)
10) Remedy for Banking Crisis	a) Localized	Quick NPL disposal Pursue accountability	Normal NPL disposal Pursue accountability
	b) Systemic	Slow NPL disposal Fat spread	Slow NPL disposal Gov. capital injection

Source: Richard Koo, The Holy Grail of Macroeconomics: Lessons from Japan's Great Recession, John Wiley & Sons, Singapore, 2008

driven by ordinary business cycles and another by balance sheet problems. In the first case, where private-sector balance sheets remain fundamentally sound, monetary easing is the correct policy response. But in the latter case, where devastated private-sector balance sheets are in need of repair, fiscal stimulus becomes essential.

If John Maynard Keynes had written in 1936 that fiscal stimulus should be used only when the private sector is minimizing debt despite near-zero interest rates, his policy recommendations would not have been abused during the 1950s and 1960s and his theories would not have been discredited. Similarly, if Milton Friedman and his followers had realized that the linkage between central bank action and economic activity is valid only when the private sector has a clean balance sheet and is maximizing profits, many countries experiencing a balance sheet recession would not have wasted precious time tinkering with monetary policy when what they needed was a fiscal response.

Once economic textbooks come to draw a distinction between the two types of recession, policymakers will not have to deal with the contradictory policy recommendations they face today because the general public will understand that fiscal stimulus is necessary when the private sector is minimizing debt at near-zero interest rates. Until then, however, policymakers must fight an uphill battle against the orthodoxy to implement and sustain the required fiscal stimulus while explaining to the public that the economy is afflicted with a different kind of disease requiring a different kind of treatment.

CHAPTER 5

Economic Integration and Global Crises: A Perspective from the Developing World

Jayati Ghosh

Decoupling?

It is now commonplace to note that global production and trade structures have changed substantially in the recent decades of greater global integration, and particularly since the turn of the century. The past two decades have been seen as the period of "emergence" of some developing countries as major exporters and importers, as well as new sources of foreign capital flows. This is widely perceived to have significant implications for existing trade structures and patterns, as well as for global power as expressed in other ways.

For example, according to data of the United Nations Statistical Department (National Accounts Main Aggregates), in 2000 Western Europe and North America accounted for nearly two-thirds (64 percent) of global GDP (measured in nominal exchange rates), but by 2011 this share had fallen to less than

57 percent. Most of this shift was accounted for by the increased share of East Asia and the Pacific, which by 2011 produced nearly a quarter (24 percent) of global GDP. South Asia also increased its share, which, however, still remains fairly small at less than 4 percent. The shift was even greater in terms of manufacturing value-added: here, the share of North America and western Europe together fell from 60 percent of the global total in 1995 to well below half (47 percent) in 2011, while the share of East Asia and the Pacific went up from 24 percent to 36 percent in the same period. Changes in value-added in services have been less marked, with the North retaining its dominant share at around 64 percent in 2011. While the share of South Asia in global services output nearly doubled over the period, it was still only just below 3 percent. Figures of the World Trade Organization (WTO online database) show how this shift of global production at the margin has been reflected in the pattern of merchandise trade. Clearly, China has been the big player in this shift, most of which occurred in the 2000s. Between 2000 and 2011, China's share of total global merchandise exports increased from 3.9 percent to 10.4 percent, while its share of manufacturing exports more than tripled from 4.7 percent to 15.4 percent (incidentally nearly double the US share of 8.4 percent in that year).

All this is well-known and has given rise to popular perceptions that significant parts of the emerging world can "decouple" from advanced economies experiencing stagnation or recession. Such expectations were, however, rather quickly belied during the Great Recession of 2008–2009. The extent to which economic "fundamentals" quickly unraveled across the developing world came as a surprise to those analysts who argued that some developing countries—especially in developing Asia, and in particular

China—could not only avoid the adverse effects of the crisis, but also emerge as an alternative growth pole for the world economy. Falling exports and dramatically reversing capital flows caused economic distress in many countries and affected even the strongest of them. Even in countries like China, which were earlier seen as relatively immune, only very proactive countercyclical measures, including fiscal stimulus packages and very substantial monetary and credit easing, allowed the growth momentum to be restored.

However, this recently experienced reality has not prevented the idea of a decoupling from resurfacing in the current context. It is certainly true that in many parts of the developing world the recovery was faster and sharper than in the North. In China and India, for example, economic activity decelerated somewhat but continued to increase. By 2012 it was once again being argued that in these large countries and elsewhere the growth engine can be decoupled from the sputtering and hesitant recovery in the northern countries. Prospects for northern economies remain gloomy, driven by wrong policy choices largely determined by political forces, as the US economy is further enmeshed in politically determined fiscal constraints and the crisis in the Euro zone plays out to create chronic economic weakness and potential disaster in Europe. As it becomes clear that expecting any positive stimulus from these two large regions is misplaced, eyes are turning toward the group of the BRIC nations (Brazil, Russia, India, and China), or to the region of developing Asia, to provide other growth poles in what will otherwise be a sagging and even dismal global economic story.

To what extent are the hopes put in these countries justified? Consider the recent trends in growth: while overall GDP growth rates in emerging and developing economies remained higher than in the advanced countries, they also turned negative in the last quarter of 2008 and the first quarter of 2009. In the current global slowdown, developing countries are also affected, with continuing synchronicity of even quarterly changes between the advanced and emerging economies (figure 5.1). The divergence between the growth rates of these two groups of economies in late 2012 was still less than in 2007, at the peak of the global boom. More significantly, the direction of movement appears to be similar for both categories of countries, suggesting that the forces impelling change in the developing world as a whole are still largely determined by what is going on in northern economies.

One reason is the impact that the slowdown in the United States and Europe has on exports of developing countries. Here the story is unambiguous (figure 5.2): export growth rates of the advanced and the emerging economies tend to move in tandem.

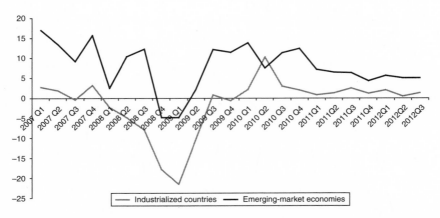

Figure 5.1 Industrialized countries and emerging market economies: quarterly GDP growth, 2007–2012. (annualized rates, percent)

Source: IMF World Economic Outlook Update, January 2013.

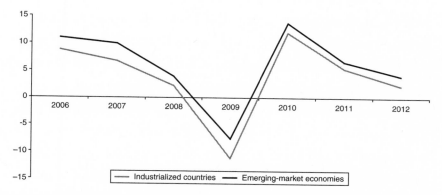

Figure 5.2   Industrialized countries and emerging market economies: change in export volume of goods and services, 2006–2012. (annual percentage change)

Source: IMF World Economic Outlook database (accessed February 19, 2013).

Very recent data for some important emerging economies such as China, Brazil, and India indicate an even sharper slowdown, suggesting that export dependence on the northern economies is still critical. And since so many countries in the region are highly trade-dependent and have generally chosen export-oriented growth as their development strategy, the slowdown in exports will necessarily also affect levels of economic activity, employment, and investment.

The continued dependence on northern markets, even as production shifts to other regions are so evident, reflects the pattern of recent economic integration. For example, much of the rapid increase in intraregional trade in developing Asia (the most dynamic region of the world in the past decade) has occurred because of the emergence of a multilocation multicountry export production network, increasingly organized around China as the country where the final processing takes place. More than half of the exports of developing Asia are within the region, but four-fifths of this trade consists of intermediate goods used for further production, rather than final demand. Such intermediate trade is obviously closely linked to the behavior of the ultimate export markets, which still remain dominantly in the North, despite recent changes in direction of trade. Thus, for example, China (which is the fulcrum of much of this kind of export-oriented activity) still looks to the United States and the European Union for just under 40 percent of its total exports and a greater proportion of its nonintermediate exports. Reduced demand from these markets obviously translates into reduced demand for raw materials and intermediates required for processing into goods for these markets. Therefore, expectations of developing Asia—or indeed other emerging economies in other parts of the world—being able to blithely withstand the latest round of economic crisis are not just overoptimistic but probably wrong.

There is no doubt that the world economy is changing and older power imbalances are shifting to newer and more complex scenarios. But a premature celebration of this tendency in most "emerging" economies without careful recognition of the realities and limitations inherent in the process is not only unjustified but can even be described as hubris. This is particularly so if growth expectations continue to rely on a development strategy that is unlikely to deliver sustained growth in future. There are at least three considerations that make the current strategy of choice (even in the "successful" developing countries) one that will be hard to sustain in the future: the impact of financial liberalization; the mercantilist obsession with export-oriented growth that generates adverse distributive consequences; and the inadequate attention to ecological imbalances that are already evident and emerge from the patterns of material expansion.

The Consequences of Financial Liberalization

It hardly needs to be reiterated that financial liberalization has resulted in an increase in financial fragility in developing countries, making them prone to periodic financial and currency crises. These relate both to internal banking and related crises, and currency crises stemming from more open capital accounts. The origin of several crises can be traced to the shift to a more liberal and open financial regime, since this unleashes a dynamic that pushes the financial system toward a poorly regulated, oligopolistic structure, with a corresponding increase in fragility. Greater freedom to undertake financial investments, including in sensitive sectors such as real estate and stock markets, the ability to increase exposure to particular sectors and individual clients and increased regulatory forbearance, all lead to increased instances of financial failure. In addition, the emergence of universal banks or "financial supermarkets" increases the degree of entanglement of different agents within the financial system and also the risk of domino effect caused by individual financial failures.

Financial markets left to themselves are known to be prone to failure because of the public goods characteristics of information that agents must acquire and process. They are characterized by insufficient monitoring by market participants. Individual shareholders tend to refrain from investing money and time in collecting information about the management and performance of companies whose stocks they acquire, hoping that others would do so instead and knowing that all shareholders, including themselves, benefit from the information garnered. As a result there may be inadequate monitoring leading to risky decisions and malpractice. Financial firms wanting to reduce or avoid monitoring costs may just follow other, possibly larger, financial firms in making their investments, leading to what has been observed as the "herd instinct" characteristic of financial players. This not merely limits access to finance for some agents, but could lead to overlending to a small number of other entities, failure of which could have systemic effects.

The prevalence of informational externalities can also create other problems. Malpractice in a particular bank leading to failure may trigger fears among depositors in other banks, resulting in a run on deposits there. Disruptions may also occur because expected private returns differ from social returns in many activities. This could result in a situation where the market undertakes unnecessary risks in search of high returns. Typical examples are lending for investments in stocks or real estate. Loans to these sectors can be at very high interest rates because the returns in these sectors can touch extremely high levels even as they tend to be volatile. Since banks accept real estate or securities as collateral, borrowing to finance speculative investments in stock or real estate can spiral. This type of activity thrives because of the belief that losses, if they occur, can be transferred to the lender through default, and lenders are confident of government support in case of a crisis. This moral hazard can feed a speculative spiral that can in time lead to a collapse of the bubble and bank failures.

Meanwhile, all too often the expected microeconomic efficiency gains are not realized. In developing countries, the market for new stock issues is small or nonexistent except in periods of a speculative boom. Deregulated bank lending tends to privilege risky high-return investment rather than investment in the commodity producing sectors like manufacturing and agriculture. This tends to generate housing and personal finance booms, which in many circumstances tends to increase the fragility of the system too.

Another result of financial liberalization in imperfect markets is the strengthening of oligopolistic power through the association of financial intermediaries with nonfinancial corporations. Financial intermediaries that are part of these conglomerates allocate credit in favor of companies belonging to the group, which is by no means a more efficient allocation of finance than what could have occurred under directed-credit policies of the government. Moreover, it may well be that financial liberalization has encouraged new kinds of financial savings, but total domestic savings typically have not increased, and to the extent that there was an expansion of available financial savings, it was often the result of an inflow of foreign capital. Nor does liberalization necessarily result in intermediation of financial assets with long-term maturities; the maturity of deposits and loans is mostly less than six months. And despite short booms in stock markets, there tends to be relatively little mobilization of new capital for existing firms or of capital for new ventures. In fact, small investors tend to withdraw from markets because of allegations of manipulation and fraud, and erstwhile areas of long-term investments supported by state intervention tend to disappear. Not surprisingly, there are typically few signs of either increased volume or more efficient allocation of investment in these circumstances.

External financial liberalization, with associated capital inflows, only aggravates the consequences of liberalization and deregulation of domestic financial systems. Indeed, all the evidence on capital inflows and subsequent crises suggest that once an emerging market is "chosen" by financial markets as an attractive destination, this sets in motion processes that are likely to culminate in crisis. This works through the effects of a surge of capital inflows on exchange rates (unless the capital inflow ends up as an addition to the country's foreign exchange reserves rather than being utilized in domestic expenditure).

An appreciating real exchange rate encourages investment in nontradable sectors, the most obvious being real estate, and in domestic asset markets generally. At the same time, the upward movement of the currency discourages investment in the production of tradables and therefore contributes to a process of relative decline in real economic sectors, and possibly even deindustrialization in developing countries. Given the differential in interest rates between domestic and international markets and the lack of prudence on the part of international lenders and investors, local agents borrow heavily abroad to directly or indirectly invest in the property and stock markets. Thus, it was not by accident that all the emerging market economies experiencing substantial financial capital inflows also at a similar time experienced property and real estate booms, as well as stock market booms, even while the real economy may have been stagnating or even declining. These booms in turn generated the incomes to keep domestic demand and growth in certain sectors rising at relatively high rates. This soon resulted in macroeconomic imbalances, not in the form of rising fiscal deficits of the government, but a current account deficit reflecting the consequences of debt-financed private profligacy.

However, once the financial system of a developing country experiences a growing exposure to internationally mobile finance capital, any factor that suggests an economic or political setback in the destination country or a policy change abroad can trigger a reversal of the capital flows. And the current account deficits that are necessarily associated with capital account surpluses (unless there is large reserve accumulation) eventually create a pattern whereby the trend becomes perceived as an unsustainable one, in which any factor, even the most minor or apparently irrelevant one, can trigger a crisis of sudden outflows.

One very common conclusion that has been constantly repeated since the start of the Asian crisis in mid-1997 is the importance of "sound" macroeconomic policies once financial flows have been liberalized. It has been suggested that many emerging markets have faced problems because they allowed their current account deficits to become too large, reflecting too great an excess of private domestic investment over private savings. This belated realization is a change from the earlier obsession with government fiscal deficits as the only macroeconomic imbalance worth caring about, but it still misses the basic point. This point is that, with completely unbridled capital flows, it is no longer possible for a country to control the amount of capital inflow or outflow, and both movements can have undesirable consequences. If, for example, a country is suddenly chosen as a preferred site for foreign portfolio investment, this can lead to huge inflows, which in turn cause the currency to appreciate, thus encouraging investment in nontradables rather than tradables, and altering domestic relative prices and therefore incentives. Simultaneously, unless the inflows of capital are (wastefully) stored up in the form of accumulated foreign exchange reserves, they must necessarily be associated with current account deficits.

Large current deficits are therefore by-products of a surge in capital inflow, and that is the basic macroeconomic problem. This means that any country that does not exercise some sort of control or moderation over private capital inflows can be subject to very similar pressures. These then create the conditions for their own eventual reversal, when the current account deficit is suddenly perceived to be too large or unsustainable. In other words, once there are completely free capital flows and completely open access to external borrowing by private domestic agents, there can be no "prudent" macroeconomic policy; the overall domestic balances or imbalances will change according to the behavior of capital flows, which will themselves respond to the economic dynamics that they have set into motion.

These point to the futility of believing that capital account convertibility accompanied by domestic prudential regulation will ensure against boom-bust volatility in capital markets. Financial liberalization and the behavior of fluid finance have created a new problem, which is analogous to the old "Dutch disease," with capital inflows causing an appreciation of the real exchange rate that causes changes in the real economy and therefore generating a process that is inherently unsustainable over time.

The most forceful critique of financial liberalization relates to the observation that it creates a strong bias toward deflationary macroeconomic policies; it forces the state to adopt a deflationary stance to appease financial interests. To begin with, the need to attract internationally mobile capital means that there are limits to the possibilities of enhancing taxation, especially the taxation of capital assets and related transactions and incomes. Typically, prior or simultaneous trade liberalization has already reduced the indirect tax revenues of states undertaking financial liberalization, and so tax-GDP ratios often deteriorate in the wake of such liberalization. This then imposes limits on government spending, since finance capital is generally opposed to large fiscal deficits. This not only affects the possibilities for countercyclical macroeconomic policies but also reduces the scope for developmental or growth-oriented activities of the government.

Financial interests are against deficit-financed spending by the state for a number of reasons. To start with, deficit financing is seen to increase the liquidity overhang in the system, and therefore as being potentially inflationary. Inflation is anathema to finance since it erodes the real value of financial assets. Second, since government spending is "autonomous" in character, the use of debt to finance such autonomous spending is seen as introducing into financial markets an arbitrary player whose behavior is not driven by the profit motive and whose activities can render interest rate differentials that determine financial profits more unpredictable. If deficit spending leads to a substantial build-up of the state's debt and interest burden, it is possible that the government may intervene in financial markets to lower interest rates with implications for financial returns. Financial interests wanting to guard against that possibility tend to oppose deficit spending. Finally, since financial interests privilege the role of markets, the presence of the state as regulator and the interventionist activity of the state can be seen as inhibiting the functioning of markets and thereby affect the social legitimacy of purely market-driven processes.

These tendencies affect real investment in two ways. First, if speculative bubbles lead to financial crises, they squeeze liquidity and increase the costs of current transactions, result in distress sales of assets, and cause deflation that adversely impacts on employment and living standards. Second, in as much as the maximum returns to productive investment in agriculture and manufacturing are limited; there is a limit to what firms are willing and able to pay for the financing of such investment. Thus, despite the fact that social returns of agricultural and manufacturing investment are higher than those of stocks and real estate, and despite the contribution that such investment can make to overall growth and poverty alleviation, credit at the required amount may not be available.

This is why it is increasingly recognized that liberalization can dismantle the very financial structures that are crucial for economic growth. While the relationship between financial structure, financial growth, and overall economic development is complex, the basic issue of financing for development is really a question of mobilizing or creating real resources. In the old development literature, the issue of finance was considered only in the context of the ability of the state to tax away a part of the surplus to finance its development expenditures, and the obstacles to deficit-financed spending, given the possible inflationary consequences if real constraints to growth were not overcome. By and large, the financial sector was seen as adjusting to the requirements of the real sector.

In the brave new world, however, when the financial sector is increasingly left unregulated or covered by a minimum of regulation, market signals determine the allocation of investible resources and therefore the demand for and the allocation of savings intermediated by financial enterprises. Insufficient regulation of financial markets can result in the problems conventionally associated with a situation where private rather than overall social returns determine the allocation of savings and investment. It aggravates the inherent tendency in markets to direct credit to projects that may appear to be profitable for individual investors, but are import-intensive and do not contribute to longer-term development objectives. It also tends to concentrate investible funds in the hands of a few large players and to direct savings to already well-developed centers of economic activity. The socially desirable role of financial intermediation therefore becomes muted. This certainly affects employment-intensive sectors such as agriculture and small-scale enterprises, where the transaction costs of lending tend to be high, risks are many, and collateral not easy to ensure. The agrarian crisis in most parts of the developing world is at least partly, and often substantially, related to the decline in the access of peasant farmers to institutional finance, which is the direct result of financial liberalization. Measures that have reduced directed credit toward farmers and small producers have contributed to rising costs, greater difficulty of accessing necessary working capital for cultivation and other activities, and reduced the economic viability of cultivation, thereby adding directly to rural distress. In India, for example, the deep crisis of the cultivating community has been associated with a proliferation of farmers' suicides and other evidence of distress such as mass migrations and even hunger deaths in different parts of rural India. There is strong evidence that this has been related to the decline of institutional credit, which has forced farmers to turn to private moneylenders and involved them once more in interlinked transactions to their substantial detriment.

It also has a negative impact on any medium-term strategy of ensuring growth in particular sectors through directed credit, which has been the basis for the industrialization process through much of the twentieth century. In a large number of developing countries in the past, the financial structure was developed keeping in mind its developmental instrumentality. Financial structures were therefore created to deal with the difficulties associated with late industrial entry: capital requirements for entry in most areas were high, because technology for factory production had

evolved in a capital-intensive direction from its primitive industrial revolution level; competition from established producers
meant that firms had to concentrate on production for a protected domestic market or be supported with finance to survive
long periods of low capacity utilization during which they could
find themselves a foothold in world markets. Not surprisingly,
therefore, most late industrializing countries created strongly regulated and even predominantly state-controlled financial markets
aimed at mobilizing savings and using the intermediary function
of these markets to influence the size and structure of investment. This they did through directed credit policies and differential interest rates, and the provision of investment support to
the nascent industrial class in the form of equity, credit, and low
interest rates. By dismantling these structures financial liberalization destroys an important instrument that historically evolved in
late industrializers to deal with the difficulties of ensuring growth
through the diversification of production structures that international inequality generates. This implies that financial liberalization is likely to have depressing effects on growth through means
other than just the deflationary macroeconomic policy bias it
introduces into countries opting for such liberalization.

This is all the more significant because the process of financial
liberalization across the globe has not generated greater net flows
of capital into the developing world, as was expected by its proponents. Rather, for the past several years, net capital flows have
been in the reverse direction. Even the emerging markets that have
been substantial recipients of capital inflows have not experienced
increases in aggregate investment rates as a consequence, but have
built up their external reserves. This is only partly because of precautionary measures to guard against possible financial crises;

it also indicates a macroeconomic situation of ex ante excess of savings over investment resulting from the deflationary macro-economic stance. The curious workings of international financial markets have actually contributed to international concentration, whereby developing countries (particularly those in Asia) hold their reserves in US Treasury bills and other safe securities, and thereby contribute to the fact that the US economy continues to absorb the bulk of the world's savings. At the same time, developing countries are losing in terms of seignorage costs of holding these reserves, as typically the reserves are invested in very low-yielding "safe" assets while capital inflows include debt-creating flows at much higher rates of interests. This inverse and unde-sirable form of financial intermediation is in fact a direct result of the financial liberalization measures that have simultaneously created deflationary impulses and increased financial fragility across the developing world.

A further—and potentially even more adverse—implication of financial liberalization relates to the effects of financial spec-ulation in commodity futures markets, which has exacerbated volatility in the global prices of essential goods such as food and fuel.

Limits to the Strategy

Both the boom that preceded the crisis and the evolution of the crisis thus far have been associated with significantly increased inequality—between countries and within a significant num-ber of countries. Recent economic growth has been associated with and even depended on the greater power of capital (both multinational and domestic), reflected in rising shares of profit and interest incomes in total national income. Governments have not seen higher wages, more employment, and better working conditions as economic policy priorities, but rather as eventual by-products of the growth process. Unfortunately, in many economies, income growth has not necessarily been accompanied by more good-quality employment. Also, this profit-led growth is not sustainable beyond a point, as has become increasingly evident in the past few years. These poor employment outcomes (which also included higher rates of open unemployment in the pastcrisis trajectory) were the result of deflationary policies on the part of the governments of these countries, which sought to suppress domestic consumption and investment. The "excess savings" that were generated as a result were then stored as foreign exchange reserves—partly as insurance again future crises and partly to prevent exchange rate appreciation that would damage the export-driven model. This obviously had effects on current levels of economic activity relative to the potential. But it also negatively affected future growth prospects because of the long-term losses of potential production and income as a result of insufficient real investment, including infrastructure investment, and inadequate public services.

The export-driven model of growth came to be seen as the most successful strategy, driven by the success of China and Germany in particular. The model, sought to be emulated by almost all developing countries, was associated with a policy to keep wage costs low and to suppress domestic consumption in the attempt to remain internationally competitive and increase shares in global markets. Managing exchange rates to remain competitive, despite either current account surpluses or capital inflows, was a central element of this strategy. This was associated with the peculiar situation of rising savings rates and falling investment rates in many developing countries, and to the holding of international reserves that were then sought to be placed in safe assets abroad. This is a classic dilemma of a mercantilist strategy: such economies are forced to finance the deficits of those countries that would buy their products, through capital flows that sustain the demand for their own exports, even when those countries have a per capita income that is significantly higher than their own.

The strategy also generated fewer jobs than a more labor-intensive pattern based on expanding domestic demand would have done, which meant that employment increased relatively little despite often dramatic rises in aggregate output. This is why globally the previous boom was associated with the South subsidizing the North: through cheaper exports of goods and services, through net capital flows from developing to industrialized countries, to the United States in particular, and through flows of cheap labor in the form of short-term migration. Despite the current fragile recovery, such a strategy is unsustainable beyond a point, especially when a number of relatively large economies seek to use it at the same time.

In the precrisis boom, domestic demand tended to be profit-driven, based on high and growing profit shares in the economy and significant increases in the income and consumption of newly "globalized" middle classes, which led to bullish investment in certain nontradable sectors—for example, financial assets and real estate—and in luxury goods and services. This enabled economies to keep growing even though agriculture was in crisis and employment did not expand enough to absorb the rapidly growing labor force.

The patterns of production and consumption that emerged meant that growth also involved rapacious and ultimately destructive exploitation of the environment. The costs—in terms of excessive congestion, environmental pollution, and ecological degradation—are already becoming evident in most developing societies, not to mention the implications in terms of the forces generating climate change. The ecological constraints on such growth are already being felt, most unfairly, among those regions and people that have gained the least from the overall expansion of incomes.

There have been other negatives associated with the growth pattern. Within developing Asia, it has led to an internal "brain drain" with adverse implications for future innovation and productivity growth. The skewed structure of incentives generated by the explosive growth of finance directed the best young minds toward careers that promised quick rewards and large material gains rather than into painstaking but socially necessary occupations in research and basic science. The impact of relocation of certain industries and the associated requirement for skilled and semiskilled labor led to increased opportunities for educated employment, but it also led bright young people to enter into work that is typically mechanical and does not require much originality or creativity, with little opportunity to develop their intellectual capacities in such jobs.

At the same time, crucial activities that are necessary for the economy were inadequately rewarded. Farming in particular became increasingly fraught with risk and subject to growing volatility and declining financial viability, while nonfarm work did not increase rapidly enough to absorb the labor force even in the fastest growing economies of the region.

This strategy bred and increased global inequality, and also sowed the seeds of its own destruction for both external and internal reasons. Externally, deficit countries will either choose or be forced to reduce their deficits through various means, including protectionist responses. Internally, suppression of wage incomes and domestic consumption will meet with political resistance. In either case, the pressures to find more sustainable sources of economic growth, particularly through domestic demand and wage-led alternatives, are likely to increase. So countries must diversify their sources of growth, looking for other export markets as well as for internal engines of growth.

Policy Responses to the Current Global Crisis

Two major misreadings of economic policy requirements have combined to intensify the ongoing global crisis. The first is the notion that the immediate concern should be the reduction of public debt and fiscal deficits. In fact, worsening fiscal imbalances in most major economies were a *result* of the 2008 financial crisis, not a cause of it, as automatic stabilizers and fiscal stimulus packages came into play. It is already evident that fiscal tightening in stressed economies is self-defeating. By reducing GDP growth and thereby fiscal revenues, it makes economic recovery more difficult and is counterproductive in terms of improving fiscal indicators. It is difficult, if not impossible, to reduce debt-to-GDP ratios in a period when the rate of interest on the public debt far exceeds the nominal growth rate (as currently in the southern European crisis economies). Further, the fact that countries running large current-account surpluses show no willingness to compensate for the imbalance by encouraging more domestic expenditure (especially in the form of public spending) bodes ill for global growth prospects. What will drive growth—globally and nationally—when countries (even those with external surpluses) persist in following austerity programs that cut incomes and demand?

The second major misreading is an overoptimistic assessment of the self-correcting powers of financial markets. It has meant that thus far attempts to reregulate financial markets have been limited and halting. Financial deregulation led to a large, opaque, and undercapitalized "shadow banking system." It also led to a concentration of traditional banking in a few institutions that have become "too big to fail" and to increased systemic risk. Postcrisis, governments' lender-of-last-resort support to the financial system has even extended to the shadow banking system, creating massively increased moral hazard. Global commodity markets have also been affected by financial speculation, causing food and fuel prices to spiral with grave consequences for people across the world. This context makes strong reregulation of finance urgent and essential. Controls have to be tighter on the "too-big-to-fail" institutions; "shadow banking" institutions need to be covered so as to avoid regulatory arbitrage; and a macro-prudential dimension, with anticyclical capital requirements and capital controls, needs to be incorporated. But reregulation alone will not orient credit to real investment or make it accessible to small and medium-sized firms. So there must be restructuring of the financial system: giant institutions must be downsized; the activities of commercial and investment banking should be clearly separated, in order to reduce the risk of contagion; and the aim should be more diverse financial systems, with a bigger role for public and cooperative institutions. Commodity markets, which have been subject to wild price swings generated by speculative and herd behavior, need to be made more transparent, with controls on financial activity in these markets and direct intervention when required to curb price bubbles and prevent sharp declines.

However, it is not just the crisis that has emphasized the urgent need for a shift in economic strategy. The need for a major reconsideration of macroeconomic strategies is even evident in the experience of the previous boom and of the performance of "successful" economies.

It is now a cliché that every crisis is also an opportunity. Of course, as the global financial crisis continues to unfold and create downturns in real economies everywhere, it is easy to see only the downside, as jobs are lost, the value of financial savings of workers is wiped out, and material insecurity becomes widespread. But in fact this global crisis offers a greater opportunity than we have had for some time now for the developing world's citizens and their leaders to restructure economic relations in a more democratic and sustainable way.

Such restructuring must comprise several elements. Globally, everyone now recognizes the need to reform the international financial system, which has failed to meet two obvious requirements: preventing instability and crises, and transferring resources from richer to poorer economies. Not only have we experienced much greater volatility and propensity to financial meltdown across emerging markets and now even industrial countries, but even the periods of economic expansion have been based on the global poor subsidizing the rich. Within national economies, this system has encouraged procyclicality; it has rendered national financial systems opaque and impossible to regulate; it has encouraged bubbles and speculative fervor rather than real productive investment for future growth; it has allowed for the proliferation of parallel transactions through tax havens and loose domestic controls; it has reduced the crucial developmental role of directed credit. Given these problems, there is no alternative to systematic state regulation and control of finance. Since private players will inevitably attempt to circumvent regulation, the core of the financial system—banking—must be protected, and this is possible only through social ownership. Therefore, some degree of socialization of banking (and not, as in the past, just socialization of the risks inherent in finance) is also inevitable. In developing countries this is also important because it enables public control over the direction of credit, without which no country has industrialized.

Second, the obsessively export-oriented model that has dominated the growth strategy of most developing countries for the past few decades needs to be reconsidered. This is not just a desirable shift—it has become a necessity given the obvious fact that the United States cannot be expected to act as the engine of world growth through increasing import demand in the near future. This means that developing countries in general, and particularly those in developing Asia that still rely on the United States and the European Union as their primary export markets, must seek to redirect their exports to other countries and, most of all, to redirect their economies toward higher domestic demand. The latter requires a shift toward wage-led growth, particularly in economies that are large enough to sustain this shift. This can happen not only through direct redistributive policies but also through public expenditure to provide more basic goods and services.

Third, this means that fiscal policy and public expenditure must be brought back to center stage. Clearly, fiscal stimulation is now essential in both developed and developing countries to cope with the adverse effects of the current crisis on the real economy and to prevent economic activity and employment from falling. Fiscal expenditure is also required to undertake and promote investment to manage the effects of climate change and promote greener technologies. And public spending is crucial to advance the development project in the South and fulfill the promise of achieving minimally acceptable standards of living for everyone in the developing world. Social policy—the public responsibility for meeting social and economic rights of citizens—is not only desirable in its own right but it also contributes positively to economic development.

Fourth, there have to be conscious attempts to reduce economic inequalities, both between countries and within countries. We have clearly crossed the limits of what is "acceptable" inequality in most societies, and future policies will have to reverse this trend. Globally and nationally, we have to recognize the need to reduce inequalities in income and wealth, and also most significantly in the consumption of natural resources. This is even more complicated than might be imagined, because unsustainable patterns of production and consumption are now deeply entrenched in the richer countries and are aspired to in developing countries. But many millions of citizens of the developing world still have poor or inadequate access to the most basic conditions of decent life, such as minimum physical infrastructure including electricity, transport and communication links, sanitation, health services, nutrition, and education. Ensuring universal provision of these facilities will inevitably require greater per capita use of natural resources and more carbon emission. So both sustainability and equity require a reduction of the excessive resource use of the rich, especially in developed countries but also among the elites in the developing world. This means that redistributive fiscal and other economic policies must be specially oriented toward reducing inequalities of resource consumption, globally and nationally. For example, within countries essential social and developmental expenditure can be financed by taxes that penalize resource-wasteful expenditure.

Fifth, this requires new patterns of both demand and production. This is why the recent focus on developing new means of measuring genuine progress, well-being, and quality of life are so important. Quantitative GDP growth targets, which still dominate the thinking of policy makers, are not simply distracting from these more important goals, but can even be counterproductive. For example, a chaotic, polluting, and unpleasant system of privatized urban transport involving many private vehicles and overcongested roads actually generates more GDP than a safe, efficient, and affordable system of public transport that reduces vehicular congestion and provides a pleasant living and working environment. So it is not enough to talk about "cleaner, greener technologies" to produce goods that continue to be consumed according to the same old and now discredited pattern of consumption. Instead, we must think creatively about such consumption itself, and work out which goods and services are more necessary and desirable for our societies.

Sixth, this cannot be left to market forces, since the international demonstration effect and the power of advertising will continue to create undesirable wants and unsustainable consumption and production. But public intervention in the market cannot be knee-jerk responses to constantly changing short-term conditions. Instead, planning—not in the sense of the detailed planning that destroyed the reputation of command regimes, but strategic thinking about the social requirements and goals for the future—is absolutely essential. Fiscal and monetary policies, as well as other forms of intervention, will have to be used to redirect consumption and production toward these social goals, to bring about such shifts in socially created aspirations and material wants, and to reorganize economic life to be less rapacious and more sustainable.

This is particularly important for the quality of life in urban areas: the high rates of urbanization in developing countries mean that in many populous countries more than half the population already live in urban areas. Yet, because systematic urban planning for the future to make cities pleasant or livable for most residents is still so rare, there is a tendency toward urban monstrosities of congestion, inequality, and insecurity.

Seventh, since state involvement in economic activity is now an imperative, we should be thinking of ways to make such involvement more democratic and accountable within our countries and internationally. Large amounts of public money will be used for financial bailouts and the provision of fiscal stimuli, and how this is done will have huge implications for income distribution, access to resources and the living conditions of the ordinary people whose taxes will be paying for this. So it is essential that we redesign the global economic architecture so that it functions more democratically. And it is even more important that states across the world, when formulating and implementing economic policies, are more open and responsive to the needs of the majority of their citizens.

Finally, we need an international economic framework that is supportive to such change. In this regard, better control and regulation of capital flows to assure that they do not destabilize any of these strategies are important, but they are not sufficient. The global institutions that form the organizing framework for international trade, investment, and production decisions also need to change; they have to become not just more democratic in structure but more genuinely democratic and people-oriented in spirit, intent, and functioning. Financing for development and conservation of global resources must become the top priorities of the global economic institutions, which means in turn that they cannot continue to base their approach on a completely discredited and unbalanced economic model.

CHAPTER 6

Act Now! The Manifesto: A New Agenda for Global Economic Policies

Jayati Ghosh

Appropriate measures must urgently be taken to revive the world economy! Neoliberalism has failed. A return to nationalism and competition among nations must be prevented. International policy cooperation must be strengthened. It is imperative to put an end to fiscal austerity!

1. *The world economy is in its most difficult situation since the 1930s.*

   - The US, Japanese, and European economies are in deep crisis. Almost five years after the onset of the financial crisis, recovery is still out of sight. Growing poverty and high unemployment clearly show that the neoliberal agenda has failed dramatically. Attempts to make labor markets more flexible and to improve the competitiveness of nations have led to an international race to the bottom. As a result, inequality has grown dramatically and the perspectives of an entire generation have darkened. High youth unemployment and the loss of confidence in chances for social advancement provide a breeding ground for extremism that is threatening democracy.

• The financial crisis of 2008 was the result of excessive deregulation and liberalization that have turned many financial markets into casinos, with enormous new risks for the world economy. As the process of deleveraging began, governments had to bail out overindebted global players, with the result of growing public debt. The immediate impact of the financial crisis on the real economy was dampened by the rapid implementation of countercyclical policies. But this policy stance was short-lived. By now, misguided fiscal austerity has become a major threat for large parts of the world economy. A return to deep recession and even a depression can no longer be excluded.

• Developing countries and even the large emerging-market economies are still lacking the necessary strength to be able to decouple over a longer period of time from the industrialized countries. In a few countries, governments successfully followed independent and alternative policy approaches. But cases in which the right course of policy could be maintained over a longer period have been rare, due to the unequal distribution of income and economic power. One major exception is China, which achieved outstanding success over the past decades. Its government has realized that dynamic growth can be sustained only when inequality is reduced and workers obtain their fair share of the growing income. Considerable real wage increases in China over the past ten years have helped to stimulate domestic consumption and to correct external imbalances.

- Regrettably, most of the smaller and poorer developing countries continue to be highly dependent on primary commodities and on the economic performance of the industrialized countries. They have thus been unable to build their own independent policymaking competence. Moreover, only a small number of countries have been able to design and pursue independent development strategies at both the micro and the macro level. And to the extent that such countries rely on external financing, they have been paralyzed by misguided neoclassical recipes imported from the North. This holds true for labor market policies in particular. In this regard there still is a lack of comprehension of the fact that reducing inequality and encouraging participation of all members of society are important factors for sustained growth and prosperity.

2. *The financial crisis was not inevitable; nor is the looming crisis of the real economy.*
   - Both are man-made. Both are consequences, direct and indirect, of a flawed economic doctrine that has seen a revival over the past 30 years. The important lessons of the Great Depression have been forgotten or discredited. In particular, as Paul Davidson shows in this book, the significance of objective uncertainty and the consequent need for the state to assume a key role in economic stabilization are not well understood. The main fallacies of this doctrine lie in the following propositions:
   - Financial markets are efficient. If they are allowed to operate with a minimum of regulation they will maximize

their efficiency and advance economic development and prosperity. Economic agents and financial actors use all available information rationally, so that markets rapidly find stable equilibrium prices.

- The labor market operates in the same way as any goods market. Thus, there is no need for intervention in the labor market when the balance of power changes as a result of growing unemployment. The only condition for reducing unemployment is flexibility in employment conditions and wage setting mechanisms. Thus, labor market flexibility is also in the interest of workers. Moreover, wage reduction is a key instrument to respond to globalization pressures in the richer countries and to sustain the willingness of local firms to create new jobs.

- Monetary policy has the capacity to respond flexibly and effectively to any crisis, provided that central banks' decision-making is independent of political interference. Autonomy of central banks ensures price stability as the money supply will be adjusted to the objective needs of the economy. This way policy-induced inflation to reduce a large public debt will be prevented.

- Proactive fiscal policies are dangerous as they cause distortions in factor allocation and lead to inefficiency. Governments do not have the competence and information required to improve the complex process of price formation. Even investment in infrastructure is carried out better and more efficiently by the private sector. Privatization of all spheres of life will lead to an optimal relationship between the state and the market. High taxes are a threat to the economy as they reduce the propensity to invest and entrepreneurial motivation; hence the process of income creation is slowed even before these taxes can be perceived. Government intervention generally impacts negatively on the economy. The public debt has to be minimized because government borrowing is crowding out private investors in capital markets, so that the overall outcome will be suboptimal.

3. *All these propositions have been disseminated forcefully with considerable financial support. However, a closer look reveals that they are fundamentally flawed:*

- Financial liberalization and deregulation have produced greater instability and massive distortions in factor allocation. The financial crisis of 2008 has clearly shown that financial markets tend to overshoot and are systematically mispricing financial assets. Since these markets are dominated by herd behavior they do not have the capacity to fulfill the complex task of generating correct information as the neoliberal doctrine suggests. The US subprime bubble and its ramifications and side effects have amply demonstrated that financial markets tend to delink themselves from economic reality. They are betting on excessive price movements—with fatal economic repercussions, as James Galbraith shows in this volume. The same holds for other parts of the financial system. Given the empirical evidence of the past few years, there can be no doubt that foreign exchange markets are inherently unstable and tend to drive exchange rates into the opposite direction of what is warranted by fundamentals. This is because carry trade speculation based on interest rate differentials leads to an appreciation of the currencies of high-interest and high-inflation economies. Moreover, the financialization of commodity markets has caused primary commodity prices to behave in the same way as prices of purely financial products. Delinking commodity prices from physical supply and demand can create considerable damage as suppliers and consumers are no longer able to plan rationally.

- Labor markets, too, are unstable, as Heiner Flassbeck shows in his contribution to this volume. This is substantiated by the fact that following the financial crisis unemployment has risen to the highest level in more than 50 years even though the wage share is lower than any time in postwar history. This evidence contradicts the propositions of neoclassical employment theory. The reason is obvious: falling wages result in falling demand for consumer goods. A substitution of capital by labor as a result of falling wages will not take place in reality, because the immediate reduction of demand will worsen the economic environment for producers, who have to cut their output. The main flaw in neoclassical labor market theory is the neglect of the negative demand effect of falling wages. Currently, this is forcefully demonstrated by developments in southern Europe, where the slump in domestic demand deepens the crisis. At the same time, it is impossible that all countries improve their international competitiveness by wage compression. Policies that nevertheless aim at wage reduction or competitive currency devaluation involve the risk of a deflationary spiral and a race to the bottom that may end in a depression. A return to normal cyclical patterns will not be possible as long as wage earners do not share commensurately in the overall progress of the economy. The latter would require nominal wage adjustments at a rate that is in line with productivity growth plus the inflation target. Recovery from the effects of the financial crisis has come to a premature end because in an environment of high unemployment combined with extremely low wages income expectations of consumers are not favorable and negatively impact on their demand.

- In the present situation monetary policy alone does not have the capacity to provide sufficient stimulus for the global economy to recover. With negative income expectations consumption growth will not resume, and due to falling capacity utilization firms will not invest, even though they may often realize high profit margins. Central banks cannot systematically lower interest rates below zero. As the crisis continues and the risk of deflation remains, they have largely exhausted their room for maneuver. Even the commitment of keeping interest rates at extremely low levels for several years is insufficient to restore consumer and investor confidence.

- As Richard Koo shows, a proactive and expansionary fiscal policy is indispensable in a situation where all private actors aim at improving their balance sheets by reducing their indebtedness or increasing their savings. Under this constellation the state cannot attain its budgetary objective and reduce its own debt or its share in overall economic activity, no matter what the size of the public debt may be. The state therefore has to assume the role of "consumer and investor of last resort." It is a grave mistake, especially in Europe and the United States, to make public policy dependent on the degree of indebtedness of the public sector, whatever its origin may be. In large economies that are relatively closed attempts to reduce the public debt without paying due attention to the plans and behavior of private actors are bound to fail. Japan, the country with the highest ratio of public debt to GDP among all major industrialized economies, appears to have learned this lesson, as witnessed by its current expansionary fiscal policy stance.

4. *It is high time to radically reverse the direction of economic policies in all of the four areas referred to earlier:*

- Governments have to drastically limit the power of financial markets and also question financial market activity much more resolutely than in the past. They have to put an end to financial activities that are pure betting. Such activities involve high risks without generating any social return. The financial market is a highly sensitive system and its fragility must not be heightened further by such casino games. "Reregulation" is a broad concept, but in most cases it will be insufficient to create transparency with regard to social returns and to eliminate dangerous financial products. There is a need for a public supervisory body that admits new financial products to the market only when they generate a societal benefit and when their risk is manageable. This would be similar to what is practiced, for example, in the case of potentially harmful pharmaceuticals. Regulation is likely to lead to unsatisfactory outcomes as long as no clear line is drawn between economically productive financial activities and pure casino activity.

- Labor markets in the industrialized countries have to be reformed with a view to make them less, rather than more, flexible. Given the instability of the labor market, governments must prevent further destabilization resulting from downward pressure on wages in phases of growing unemployment as the present one. (Rising unemployment was an immediate effect of the financial crisis, but has not been caused by rising wages.) This can be achieved by governments providing guidance to wage negotiations between employers and employees or by establishing official guidelines aimed at linking nominal wages with macroeconomic variables, namely, productivity growth and the inflation target. In certain cases this may be considered impossible for institutional or political reasons; in such cases, however, one has to be aware that fiscal action has to be even more expansionary, something that is equally subject to controversy.

- In a situation of severe crisis monetary policy has to use all available instruments to counter the risk of deflation. But beyond that, there is a need in many countries, especially in Europe, to fundamentally rethink the role of monetary policy. In order to play a stabilizing role in the overall policy mix, monetary policy has to assume responsibility for investment and employment. If wage policy were to follow the guideline described earlier, the risk of inflation would practically disappear as the rate of inflation is closely correlated with the rise of unit labor costs. The central bank could then gear its interest rate policy toward the stimulation of investment. Experience has shown that concentrating the conduct of monetary policy on the sole objective of keeping inflation low, as currently practiced in Europe, is inadequate.

- At the present juncture, fiscal policy in the industrialized world must serve to counter the risk of a new recession. This can only be achieved with debt-financed fiscal measures as now envisaged in Japan. Clearly, implementing such policies requires a common effort of policymakers and the economics profession to remove the taboo surrounding public indebtedness. Fiscal deficits, both domestic and foreign, have to be seen in the respective overall macroeconomic savings/investment context. It is a fallacy to base macroeconomic management on purely microeconomic reasoning. As long as households aim at increasing their savings, high and growing public indebtedness can only be avoided if firms are pushed into new debt. In a market economy, a corporate sector that is hoarding large amounts of cash and liquid assets rather than investing in productive capacity must be considered an aberration: it suggests that either competition is not functioning (something that would equally call for state action, though of a different kind), or the balance of power in the labor market produces a pattern of income distribution that reduces the pressure on companies to innovate and invest. This is precisely the situation in which government intervention becomes indispensable, as argued earlier. Some countries running sustained current-account surpluses have systematically placed the resulting excess savings abroad. This should be prevented by a reform of the international monetary system ensuring that exchange rates truly reflect macroeconomic fundamentals. In countries running large current-account surpluses fiscal expansion is imperative in the present situation. Europe has to immediately put an end to fiscal austerity and wage compression in the deficit economies of the Euro zone.

5. *At the global level, there is an urgent need to revise macroeconomic policies at all levels in light of the failure of the neoliberal approach. Otherwise it is not only income growth and jobs that are at risk, but also the economic prosperity that has been created over decades and even worse: the democratic order of our states.*

- Young people, especially, need promising educational and professional perspectives. High youth unemployment causes considerable frustration and provides the breeding ground for political radicalism. Recent developments in some southern European countries that have resulted from continued creditor pressure on the governments of these countries are unacceptable and can no longer be tolerated. Youth unemployment of up to 50 percent in rich societies indicates that the European system of checks and balances is not working.

- Prosperity for all is not only possible—it is a condition for an economy to function well. For the market economy to bring its superiority to bear on technological progress, all social groups must share in the results of the joint effort of capital and labor. This is not just a legitimate social concern, it is an economic necessity: stable economic growth requires that income increases for all groups are commensurate with the gains from productivity that have jointly been achieved.

- Democracy can only function with a balanced distribution of power among social groups, in politics as much as in the economy. Excessive concentration of economic power tends to undermine democracy through lobbyism and other mechanisms. Therefore, full employment must remain a key objective of economic policy, and governments have to pursue it vigorously and without compromise. In the labor market, the most important of all markets, an appropriate balance of power can only be assured under the condition of full employment. Only when this condition is fulfilled and an effective public redistribution policy is in place is it possible to avoid excessive concentration of economic power that tends to distort the outcome of democratic processes.

- Clearly, it is essential that economic policy design takes account of ecological and environmental constraints to growth. Ecologically sound structural change requires a competent state, especially in those countries where economic activity in the past has had the strongest impact on the natural environment. Emaciated and weak states will be unable to meet this challenge, which requires bold intervention in the market mechanism and direct or indirect influence on the price formation process over a long time. Resources have to be reallocated in a way that protects the environment while offering positive prospects for future living standards. Such reallocation of resources does not mean the end of economic development but a change in the pattern of growth. There can be no doubt that developing countries will need external support for preserving their development potential.

Conclusion

Globalization over the past 30 years has led to closer economic integration among the different regions of the world than ever.

The international community has failed, however, to design effective global rules for this highly integrated global economy. Like a soccer match, an economy needs rules to function well. Owing to the lack of appropriate rules and regulation economic power has come to dominate over the interests of society at large. In the absence of state regulation at the global level the foundations of democracy are being undermined at the national level. Competition among nations overlaps with competition among firms, giving way to the law of the jungle rather than fostering equal rights for all nations.

The creation of an effective global legal and regulatory framework requires greater international policy coordination and a transfer of competences to multilateral institutions. One possibility to make international policy cooperation more effective is strengthening the G-20 and the introduction of rotating membership; another is the creation of a global economic council with a mandate to elaborate binding recommendations for national policies, taking into account the requirements of the global economy. So far, however, there is no political will to engage in such far-reaching cooperation. It is therefore essential for national governments to understand that national State egoism does not help in preserving or strengthening their power. On the contrary, by creating a vacuum it opens even more space for the accumulation of economic power in the hands of a few to an extent that will eventually threaten democracy.

About the Authors

Heiner Flassbeck is the director of Flassbeck-Economics, a consultancy for global macroeconomic questions (www.flassbeck-economics.de). Since 2005 he is honorary professor at the University of Hamburg. Before that he worked as a member of the staff of the German Council of Economic Advisors (1976 and 1980) and the Federal Ministry of Economics in Bonn until January 1986, before joining the German Institute for Economic Research (DIW) in Berlin as chief macroeconomist. From October 1998 to April 1999 he was appointed state secretary (vice minister) at the Federal Ministry of Finance, Bonn, where he was responsible for international affairs, the EU, and IMF. In 2000 he joined the Secretariat of the United Nations Conference on Trade and Development (UNCTAD), where he served as the director of the Division on Globalisation and Development Strategies from 2003 to December 2012. He was the principal author of the team preparing UNCTAD's annual Trade and Development Report, with specialization in macroeconomics, exchange rate policies, and international finance. Professor Flassbeck graduated from Saarland University, Germany, in April 1976 and obtained a PhD in economics from the Free University, Berlin, in July 1987.

He has authored five books in the past six years and published numerous articles on macroeconomic policy issues.

Paul Davidson is Holly Chair of Excellence, Emeritus at the University of Tennessee. He is a visiting scholar at the Schwartz Center for Economic Policy Analysis at the New School, New York City. He has taught economics at the University of Pennsylvania, the University of Tennessee, Rutgers University, Bristol University (UK), and the University of Cambridge. He is the cofounder and coeditor of the *Journal of Post Keynesian Economics*, a member of the advisory board of the Institute for New Economic Thinking and an honorary member of the Professional Risk Managers International Association. Professor Davidson has been the associate director of the Economics Division of the Continental Oil Company, a member of the Brookings Economic Panel, and a consultant to many private and public institutions, including: Western Union Telegraph Company, the Federal Trade Commission, the Joint Economic Committee of the US Congress, the Canadian Department of Consumer and Corporate Affairs, the central banks of Ecuador, Venezuela, and Uruguay, and the New York State Consumer Protection Agency. He is the author, coauthor, or editor of 22 books, and has authored more than 210 articles.

James K. Galbraith holds the Lloyd M. Bentsen Jr. Chair in Government/Business Relations at the Lyndon B. Johnson School of Public Affairs, and a professorship in government at the University of Texas at Austin. He is a senior scholar of the Levy Economics Institute of Bard College, Annandale-on-Hudson, New York, and chair of the Board of Economists for Peace and Security, a global professional network. In 2012 he was president of the Association for Evolutionary Economics. In his early career he served in several positions on the staff of the US Congress, including executive director of the Joint Economic Committee. Professor Galbraith has authored numerous books and academic articles and writes frequently for policy magazines and the general press. His latest book is *Inequality and Instability: A Study of the World Economy Just before the Great Crisis* (Oxford University Press, 2012). He holds degrees from Harvard and Yale (PhD in economics, 1981) and is a member of the Lincean Academy, the oldest honorary scientific society in the world.

Richard Koo is the chief economist of Nomura Research Institute. Tokyo. Before joining Nomura in 1984, he was an economist with the Federal Reserve Bank of New York (1981–1984), and a doctoral fellow of the Board of Governors of the Federal Reserve System (1979–1981). In addition to conducting financial market research, he has advised several Japanese prime ministers on how best to deal with Japan's economic and banking problems. Currently he is also serving as senior advisor to the Center for Strategic and International Studies (Washington DC) and as advisory board member of the Institute for New Economic Thinking (New York). Dr. Koo is the author of many books about the Japanese economy. His latest book *The Holy Grail of Macroeconomics—Lessons from Japan's Great Recession* (John Wiley & Sons, 2008) has been translated into four languages. He holds BA degrees in political science and economics from the University of California at Berkeley (1976) and an MA in economics from Johns Hopkins University (1979). From 1998 to 2010 Mr. Koo was a visiting professor at Waseda University in Tokyo.

Jayati Ghosh is professor of economics at the Centre for Economic Studies and Planning, School of Social Sciences, Jawaharlal Nehru University, New Delhi. She was educated at Delhi University, Jawaharlal Nehru University, and the University of Cambridge.

She has authored several books and more than 130 scholarly articles. In addition to her academic work, she is a regular columnist for several newspapers and journals. She was chairperson of the Commission on Farmers' Welfare in 2004 constituted by the state government of Andhra Pradesh in India, and member of the National Knowledge Commission reporting to the prime minister of India (2005–2009). Professor Ghosh is honorary executive secretary of International Development Economics Associates (www.networkideas.org). She has consulted for a large number of international organizations, including the United Nations Development Program (UNDP), the United Nations Conference on Trade and Development (UNCTAD), the United Nations Department for Economic and Social Affairs (UN-DESA), and the International Labour Organisation (ILO). In 2010, Professor Ghosh received the NordSud Prize for Social Sciences 2010 of the Fondazione Pescarabruzzo, Italy, and was awarded the ILO Decent Work Research Prize for 2010. She was also the principal author of the West Bengal Human Development Report 2004, which received the 2005 UNDP Award for excellence in analysis.

References

Davidson, P. (2009). *The Keynes Solution: The Path to Global Economic Prosperity.* New York and London: Palgrave/Macmillan.

Flassbeck, H. (2001). The Exchange Rate: Economic Policy Tool or Market Price? *UNCTAD Discussion Paper* 157, Geneva, November.

Galbraith, James K. (2006). "Maastricht 2042 and the Fate of Europe: Toward Convergence and Full Employment." *Levy Economics Institute Public Policy Brief* No. 87 (November). Published separately by the Friedrich Ebert Stiftung, International Policy Analysis Unit, March 2007.

———— (2012). *Inequality and Instability: A Study of the World Economy Just before the Great Crisis.* New York: Oxford University Press.

Galbraith, James K., and Enrique Garcilazo (2004). "Unemployment, Inequality and the Policy of Europe, 1984–2000." *Banca Nazionale del Lavoro Quarterly Review* LVII (228) (March): 3–28. Reprinted in Richard P. F. Holt and Steven Pressman, eds., *Empirical Post Keynesian Economics: Looking at the Real World.* Armonk: M.E. Sharpe, 2007, 44–69.

Hicks, J. R. (1977). *Economic Perspectives: Further Essays on Money and Growth.* Oxford: Clarendon Press.

Jing Chen and James Galbraith (2009). "A Biophysical Approach to Production Theory." *UTIP Working Paper* No. 55 (February 1). http://utip.gov.utexas.edu/papers/utip_55.pdf.

———— (2011). "Institutional Structures and Policies in an Environment of Increasingly Scarce and Expensive Resources: A Fixed Cost

Perspective." *Journal of Economic Issues* XLV (2) (June): 301–309. DOI: 10.2753/JEI0021–3624450206.

——— (2012). "Austerity and Fraud under Different Structures of Technology and Resource Abundance." *Cambridge Journal of Economics* 36 (1) (January): 335–343. DOI: 10.1093/cje/ber027.

——— (2012). "A Common Framework for Evolutionary and Institutional Economics." *Journal of Economic Issues* XLVI (2) (June): 419–428. DOI: 10.2753/JEI0021–3624460217.

Keynes, J. M. (1936). *The General Theory of Employment, Interest and Money*. London and Basingstoke: Macmillan and Cambridge University Press for the Royal Economic Society.

———(1937). "The General Theory of Employment." *The Quarterly Journal of Economics* 51 (2): 209–223.

———(1939). "*Professor* Tinbergen's Method." *The Economic Journal* 49 (195): 558–577.

Knight, F. H. (1921). *Risk, Uncertainty and Profits*. New York: Houghton Miflin.

Lucas, R., and T. J. Sargent (1981). *Rational Expectations of Econometric Practicies*. Minneapolis: University of Minnesota Press.

Machina, M. J. (1987). "Choice under Uncertainty: Problems Solved and Unsolved." *The Journal of Economic Perspectives* 1 (1): 121–154.

OECD (1994). *The OECD Jobs Study*. Paris.

Ricardo, D. (1817). *On the Principles of Political Economy and Taxation*. London: John Murray.

Samuelson, P. A. (1969). "Classical and Neoclassical Theory." In: R. W. Clower (ed.), *Monetary Theory*. London: Penguin.

Sargent, T. J. (1993). *Bounded Rationality in Mascroeconomics*. Oxford: Clarendon Press.

UNCTAD (United Nations Conference on Trade and Development) (2011). *Trade and Development Report: Post-crisis Policy Challenges in the World Economy*. New York and Geneva.

——— (2012). *Trade and Development Report: Policies for Inclusive and Balanced Growth*. New York and Geneva.